May Al-Daftari was born in Baghdad and lived in Beirut and London. Currently, she is living in Amman.

She is a graduate of the American University of Beirut (AUB) with a bachelor's degree in Economics and is a holder of master's degree in Area Studies from the School of Oriental and African Studies (SOAS), London.

She was chief editor of the Arab Gulf Journal, a biannual between 1981–1987 and a founding member and director of the British charity, Medical Aid for Iraqi Children (MAIC) from 1995 until 2009.

She is the author of *Issues in Development: The Arab Gulf States*, London 1980 and *Yassin Al-Hashimi, Biographical Recollections*, Amman 2017 (published in Arabic).

A four-year-old boy suffering from leukaemia in remission at Al Mansour Paediatric Teaching Hospital. Baghdad, September 2000.

In memory of the millions of Iraqi children who died or have been tragically scarred by the effects of sanctions and wars.

May Al-Daftari

HAS THE WORLD LOST ITS HUMANITY?

MAIC Memoirs: 1995–2009

AUSTIN MACAULEY PUBLISHERS™

LONDON • CAMBRIDGE • NEW YORK • SHARJAH

A CIP catalogue record for this title is available from the British Library.

ISBN 9781528992459 (Paperback)
ISBN 9781528992466 (Hardback)
ISBN 9781528992473 (ePub e-book)

www.austinmacauley.com

First Published (2021)
Austin Macauley Publishers Ltd
25 Canada Square
Canary Wharf
London
E14 5LQ

This book would not have been possible without the dedication of the people who helped to make Medical Aid for Iraqi Children (MAIC) what it was. This includes all the charity members in London, Iraq and Amman, as well as the British donors and supporters from all walks of life and the numerous individuals and institutions from the international community who showed genuine interest in the cause of MAIC. To them all, I express my deepest gratitude.

I am indebted to the late Dr Rula Quawas for her interest in my recollections of MAIC and her encouragement to go ahead with the project.

To my husband, Mazin, I express my love and appreciation for his insightful comments during the early days of the draft.

I am most grateful to my dear friend Miss Sirsa Hikmat, whom I cannot thank enough for patiently reading the draft at its various stages and offering useful advice.

I thank Mrs Sarah Turner profusely for her reading of the manuscript and making valuable remarks and corrections.

I also want to convey my warmest affection to my children, Lara and Ali, for their encouragement and support; and to my granddaughters, Rhea, Talia, Tara and Darya, for being my true inspiration.

Table of Contents

Epigraph

'...those who possess power without compassion, might
without morality and strength without sight.'

Martin Luther King, April 1967
**(describing political leaders as part of his opposition to
the war on Vietnam)**

Prologue

In 2008 I moved with my husband, Mazin Ali Mumtaz Al-Daftari, from London to Amman. We live at the outskirts of Amman, overlooking the Dead Sea, Jerusalem and Jericho. The drive between our home and Amman is breath-taking. You see oak and olive trees, scattered Bedouin tents and sheep grazing on the green vegetation on both sides of the road. Often the tranquillity of the scenery brings back contrasting memories of my several humanitarian trips to Bagdad representing the charity, Medical Aid for Iraqi Children (MAIC). From 1995 to 2009, I was a Trustee and Director of the charity, which provided medical supplies to children's hospitals in Iraq while the country suffered from the effects of two Gulf wars in 1991 and 2003 and from the cruel, comprehensive international sanctions imposed on Iraq by the UN in 1990 which lasted until 2003. During these years, it was impossible to get anything into the country, even the kind of basic supplies which are usually taken for granted.

The drive makes me live once again the sixteen-hour land journeys to Baghdad, when we had to drive along dangerous highways, as air travel was prohibited at the time. The only scene is an endless desert land. Flashes of images roll in my memory, of little faces in hospital wards, lying on soiled beds, in pain, deprived of basic medical requirements.

As we continue our daily drive to Amman, I often think of my MAIC colleagues in London and miss them dearly. Over the years we built strong bonds that kept us united as we faced many challenges. Together we shared intense moments of frustration as obstacles came our way, and also moments of elation, once our medical supplies safely reached their destinations, the assigned paediatric hospitals.

Equally, I remember with great respect and admiration the brave doctors in Iraq and their dedication to helping and saving children with the few medicines and equipment which were available. I also think of MAIC's Committee in Amman, who tirelessly facilitated the transit arrangements of the charity's medical supplies between London and Baghdad.

With a deep feeling of gratitude, I think of our generous donors, especially those who deprived themselves of essential necessities so that they could provide funds to help sick children in Iraqi hospitals. Remembering those touching stories of sacrifice and generosity is humbling. Those marvellous people need to be credited and their stories documented.

For the last few years, I have been going over these cherished memories and now that I have compiled these stories, I wish to share them with others.

I will also highlight certain times and events in my life which shaped my humanitarian interest, enlarged my vision and guided me in my work with the charity.

Chapter 1
Personal Background

On a sunny October morning in 2010 while sipping coffee in the garden of my new home in the outskirts of Amman, I started remembering the years I spent working for the charity Medical Aid for Iraqi Children (MAIC). It had been a year since the closure of the charity and I felt a sense of urgency to tell the story of the wonderful people I worked with, the generous hard-working supporters and the many eventful episodes I experienced during those challenging years.

On that particular day, I decided to write *MAIC Memoirs* and revisit important chapters in my early life, acknowledge the inspiring role of all the marvellous people who guided me throughout my humanitarian work with MAIC.

Consequently, my first step was to seek the advice of a dear friend, Sirsa Hikmat, instructor at the Department of English, University of Jordan. Sirsa was very encouraging and helpful and continued to advise me throughout my work on the book. At the time, she suggested I meet with Professor Rula Quawas, a colleague of hers at the same department, and arranged the meeting a few days later.

Rula had a very busy schedule and a number of projects underway, yet she was able to meet with me a few times. She listened carefully as I recounted my experience at the charity and showed deep concern for the suffering of the children I had observed. Rula also read a few pages of my notes and was very forthcoming. She encouraged me to write my recollections and look back at the events with an evaluative and interpretive sense. Unfortunately and sadly, Rula passed away in 2017 after a short illness. I feel deeply indebted to her for her valuable guidance.

My Early Life

I am nearly nine years old, sitting with my sister Sevim next to my father, Abdul Rahman Amin Ziwar, listening to him as he recounted stories about his grandmother, the famous Haybet Khatoun, who married her cousin, Ahmed Ziwar bin Abdullah. She was well known for her charitable work in her birthplace, Adhamiya district, and throughout Baghdad. My father was very proud of her and spoke of her with admiration. She helped by feeding the poor, and sponsored underprivileged families. She was well educated, had beautiful handwriting and enjoyed literature and poetry. At her home overlooking the Dijla River, she received dignitaries and intellectuals from the different Welayats which were under Ottoman rule.

In the early twentieth century, she built a charitable complex which included a mosque, a drinking fountain and a science school in 1336 Hijri. The school had special quarters for students to live in and a monthly allowance was given to each student. Learning at the school was completely free of charge. What was most interesting about the school was its sophisticated legal set up; it was a trust in today's terms. It specified Haybet Khatoun's financial commitment and assigned different responsibilities to paid staff. It also included a list of appointed and future trustees, to secure the continuity of the school in the future. Upon her death, she was buried in her school. Unfortunately, with the passing away of Zeinab Khatoun the last trustee, the project discontinued and was taken over by the Awqaf (ministry of religious affairs) and is still running today but under a different arrangement. Haybet Khatoun is still remembered in Iraq as a true philanthropist of her time. (More information on her trust is registered in the Iraqi Ministry of Awqaf, file no. 40 updated in 1393 Hijri.)

Another subject that was close to my father's heart was finding similarities between the three monolithic religions. He kept by his side the Holy Quran, the Bible and the Thawrat. I often saw him reading through the holy books, taking notes on what they had in common. He taught us to respect all religions and show concern for others.

He also encouraged me to write and asked me to present him every week with a two-page journal with pictures, drawings and a few written comments. Playing chess was a hobby close to his heart; he allowed me to watch as he played with his friends and occasionally made me move the chess pieces. I became fond of the game and now enjoy playing it whenever I have a chance.

My mother, Nigar Ali Hayder, came from a Circassian family. Her father, Ali Hayder Lutfi Pasha, was a Kabardin and her mother, Nuria Suleiman Khantou, was a Shabshigh. (Both the Kabardin and the Shabshigh are tribes from the Caucases.) My mother was raised in Istanbul and later continued her studies at the Franciscan, a French school in Damascus, before marrying my father and coming to Baghdad. She had a talent for painting and played the piano. She was a caring and loving mother and very protective of us.

The Beirut Years

A few years later, following the 1958 brutal revolution in Iraq, we moved with my parents and sister to Beirut in September 1959, where my elder brother Kanan and his family had arrived a few months earlier.

I entered the Ahliah National School for Girls in Beirut. This was an important part of my teenage life. Madame Wadad Makdisi Cortas, the headmistress of the school, was an Arabist and had great influence on me in developing my aspirations. In her morning talks before classes, she spoke to us of our Arab roots and made us proud of our culture. She regularly emphasised the importance of helping the needy and encouraged us to do charity and community work. With a few other students, I used to help young blind children from an elementary school by guiding them through musical concerts and other entertainment events. I also used to visit a sixteen-year-old visually impaired student twice a week to read his textbooks to him.

On graduation day, I was one of two graduates to give a speech. In preparation for my speech, entitled "Tagore Speaks to Us", Madame Cortas asked me to read about Rabindranath Tagore and his philosophy. He had been born in 1861 and was awarded the Nobel Prize for Literature in 1913. I based my speech on a lecture he made during his visit to an Arab country. My friend Houda Zouraq was to give the second speech and talk about Jubran Khalil Jubran, the famous Lebanese poet and writer. I remember vividly the words I quoted from Tagore's address in my speech: 'Let us work together with our brothers, regardless of our diverse beliefs, culture and religions to protect the principles of humanity.' Another quote also had an effect on me: 'To be knowledgeable of one's rich culture and learn and take from the west what compliments your culture but do not let it take over your own culture.'

Now, as I write my memoir of my work at MAIC, I realise how important those people were in my childhood and teens and what a positive effect they had on my adult life. I am most grateful and indebted to them.

After finishing high school from Ahliah, I entered the American University of Beirut (AUB) and graduated in 1966 with a Bachelor's degree in Economics. The Beirut years were some of my happiest; I got married there in 1964 to Mazin Al-Daftari the son of Ali Mumtaz Al-Daftari, who was Finance Minister of Iraq in the 1940s and 1950s. We also had our two children Lara and Ali in Beirut. Lebanon became a home to me after I left Iraq, where I formed close friendships during my high school and university years which until today I deeply cherish. It was very sad to leave this beautiful country and its wonderful people in 1975 after the civil war.

Beirut was an important Arab centre financially and intellectually. Unfortunately, the civil war in Lebanon that started in April 1975 and lasted fourteen years shattered the Lebanese dream and brought catastrophic results to the population, including secular divisions, tragic loss of life and a devastated economy. It took the country more than two decades to achieve some degree of normalisation.

The London Years

In October 1975 I moved from Beirut to London with my husband Mazin and our two children, Lara, who was eight and Ali, who was six. It was my second significant move, after moving with my parents and sister from Baghdad to Beirut in 1959.

Living in London was a new experience; it was a city of great culture and heritage and a centre for international politics and finance. In 1978, I joined the School of Oriental and African Studies (SOAS). Being a mother of two young children, attending university and studying was not an easy task. However, I was able to graduate in 1980 with a Master's degree in Area Studies and Economics.

Meanwhile, the turmoil in the Middle East was worsening; there was civil war in Lebanon, and in Palestine, we saw daily killings of Palestinians and the confiscation of their land by the Israelis. Many of us in the Arab community in London were deeply concerned about the tragic conditions in the Middle East and felt the urgent need to help. This led to the formation of new British charities to help Arab causes such as the Arab Women's Association (AWA), Give a Child a Toy and the British Lebanese Association, alongside Medical Aid for Palestinians (MAP), which was already in existence.

I served for one year as a Board member at the American University of Beirut Chapter in London (AUB Chapter) in 1981. The years between 1980 and 1990 offered me exposure and helped me to interact with my new environment.

In 1980, soon after graduating from SOAS, I started a publishing company, M.D. Research and Services Ltd, which focused on economic and social development in the Arab Gulf States. The first publication was *Issues in Development: The Arab Gulf States.* The second was *The Arab Gulf Journal*, a biannual that lasted until 1983. During my publishing years, I founded "Invest ART", a company specialising in Orientalist,

Modern British and Post-Impressionist paintings. The company was closed in 1989, following the decline of the art market. My love of art started as a hobby when I was in my early twenties and grew up with me over time. It is still one of my favourite interests.

Throughout the years I spent in London, I came to realise how charitable the British people are. There is so much to learn from them, especially their great passion for charitable causes. They have a genuine drive to help the needy wherever they are, unrestricted by race, religion or nationality. I owe a great deal to this valuable experience, which I made much use of in later years.

The Iraq–Iran War, 1980–1988

The 1980s were another dark period in Iraq's history. The Iran–Iraq war (1980–1988) had a catastrophic effect on the country, causing the deaths and injuries of one million Iraqis and severe depletion of the country's resources. During the eight years of war, travelling was prohibited, depriving millions of families from getting together.

I was parted from my mother and sister for eight years, as they had been living in Baghdad since their return from Beirut in 1965. Once the war was over in 1990, I went to visit them in Baghdad and stayed with my sister Sevim, her late husband Dr Ihsan Al Bahrani a prominent Iraqi cardiologist, and her teenage son, Shamil. My mother was already very old and sick and was living with them as my father had passed away in 1976.

Sanctions and the Gulf Wars, 1990–2003

By mid-1990 Iraq was becoming the dominant news in the media, with a lot of emphasis on Iraqi military power. Iraq invaded Kuwait on 2 August 1990, which led the United Nations to impose economic sanctions on Iraq on 6 August 1990. The sanctions regime imposed a total embargo on the country's imports and exports, froze its assets and banned Iraq from selling its oil. In all, it deprived its people of everything, even of basic necessities.

Meanwhile, there were signs from the international community led by the United States of America and Britain of a fast build-up towards war. The Iraqi population was in a state of panic and fear, not knowing where to go in the event of war. Gradually, we lost contact with our families. Telephone lines, which were our only means of communication, were cut off.

On that apocalyptic night of 17 January 1991, the first Gulf War started. Coalition forces from thirty-nine countries started bombing Iraq. A most disturbing comment was continuously repeated on CNN news channel – 'The skies of Baghdad are illuminated' – and reporters compared the bombing to the 4 July celebration, disregarding the thousands of innocent people who were killed and maimed and the millions of children who were traumatised. As we saw images of war and destruction on our screens, we thought endlessly about the likely fate of our elderly mothers and our families. CNN's inhumane and ill-considered comment still rings in my ears.

The coalition planes sprayed the country with their lethal bombs, targeting the power stations and public utilities. Water purification plants and sewage systems were heavily bombed, which led to the contamination of water supplies. The milk factory, a vital source of nutrition for babies, was also hit and destroyed. The bombing lasted for days. Mazin and I both lost contact with our families for forty days. This was one of the most painful and worrying periods in our lives. There was a complete blackout on news from them; we didn't know where they would go during the bombing or whether they had survived. My mother was bedridden, suffering from heart problems and arthritis, and it would not have been easy to move her to a safer location under the barrage of shelling. Mazin's mother, Nimat Yassin Al Hashimi, was all alone, as his father, Ali Mumtaz Al-Daftari, had passed away a few months before the war began.

Suddenly, after six weeks, we received a signal of hope, a telephone call from Wafaa Baban, a dear friend of the family, who was living in Amman. A taxi driver had brought her a short note from Mazin's mother, informing us that she and my family had survived the bombing and were safe. Many family members had left their homes and gone to separate areas for shelter. It was a long time before we could speak to our families due to the damage done to telephone lines and electricity during the bombing.

The first letter we received by hand was from my sister on 3 March 1991. It was very sad to read about what my family had gone through. She described the tragic ordeal of living in a cottage on farmland in Fahama, in the outskirts of Baghdad, that belonged to one of their close friends. There were around forty of them sharing one large space, sleeping on the floor with no electricity or water. They had to pump water from the river to drink, cook and bathe. They also shared one bathroom on the top floor, where they had to carry my frail mother every time she needed to use the facility. During the continuous shelling, my sister's daughter-in-law went into labour. It was very difficult to reach a hospital during the bombing, with no fuel to run a car. Her husband and two family members had to carry her to reach the nearest hospital. Although the hospital had no electricity and the journey was a real nightmare; she gave birth to a healthy baby boy and returned safely to the shelter with her newborn.

The bombing of Iraq reduced the country to the 'pre-industrial age', as Mr Martti Ahtisaari, the UN Under-Secretary General, described it in his report of 20 March 1991 following his visit to Iraq to assess the aftermath of the first Gulf War. He wrote, 'Nothing that we had seen or read had quite prepared us for the particular form of devastation, which has now befallen the country.' He continued: 'Iraq has, for some time to come, been relegated to a pre-industrial age.' Moreover, the combined effect of the sanctions and this ferocious war left Iraq and its people in a state of unparalleled tragedy.

In July 1991, after an agonising wait, I met my mother, sister and her family in Amman, where we spent a month together. Amman became our meeting place and refuge for the next two years. We met again in the summers of 1992 and

1993. Those reunions were a mixture of happy and emotional times. I listened to the painful stories of the war, the sanctions and the tragedies that had befallen many friends and families.

As time went by, my mother's health worsened. She was no longer able to make the agonising journey between Baghdad and Amman, which used to take sixteen hours at that time. The three years that followed were very hard on my sister. She devoted herself to nursing our bedridden mother full-time and to coping with the difficulties of life under sanctions. All basic needs for a bedridden patient were unavailable. Flights to Iraq were prohibited, which made it very difficult to send my mother her medicines and other necessities from abroad. With great difficulty, whenever we used to find a traveller going from Amman to Baghdad by road, I would send with him or her a few of the most urgent items.

During the first five years under sanctions, Iraqis were deprived of everything. Aid was provided only by a few international aid organisations such as WHO, Care, and the International Committee of the Red Cross (ICRC). One of the ICRC's urgent tasks was to repair water plants. Very few supplies of food and medicines were donated. Sanctions were applied to all the country's imports. Medicines and food were in extremely short supply. The simplest daily requirements were unavailable, such as nappies for babies, soap, cotton wool, disinfectants etc. Iraqis suffered tragically. As a result, thousands of children died and millions were undernourished.

The situation remained unchanged until April 1995, when the sanctions were reviewed and the "Oil-for-Food Programme" Resolution SCR986 was introduced. It allowed Iraq to sell limited supplies of oil and import, with its revenue, limited supplies of food and medicine, which were conditional on the approval of the UN Sanctions Committee in New York. The Resolution required that all lists of items to be imported should be sent to the Committee first to be vetted.

Forming the Charity Medical Aid for Iraqi Children (MAIC)

During these dire conditions, witnessing the suffering and agony of Iraqis, especially of children and the elderly, my passion to help Iraqi children became stronger. Earlier, after the 1991 Gulf War, I had contacted the ICRC and sent them a small donation raised from two friends and myself, earmarked for their humanitarian work in Iraq. I was later invited to visit the ICRC headquarters in Geneva, where I met with its President at the time, Dr Samaruga, and was introduced to the department in charge of the rehabilitation of Iraq. I was briefed about their humanitarian work in Iraq and we agreed to raise funds together for the ICRC project to repair the damaged water plants which had been heavily bombed during the war.

On my return to London, I held a fundraising gathering at my home, which raised £45,000 for the ICRC. Within the same year, I formed, with a group of friends, a committee to organise a fundraising lunch to benefit the ICRC. The event was held at the Grosvenor House Hotel, London on 19 October 1991 (see Appendix 1). The guest speaker was Mr Claudio Caratsch, the ICRC Vice President at the time. The event was very successful; over 350 people attended and £95,000 was raised for the ICRC.

With this experience and especially after the birth of my first granddaughter, Rhea, who became my inspiration, I decided to form a British registered charity to help Iraqi children. Rhea was born on 11 December 1991. I loved her dearly and spoiled her with toys and beautiful clothes. Yet in my mind and heart, I felt deep sadness and a sense of guilt as I thought of the millions of children in Iraq who were deprived of everything, even of milk and the simplest necessities for their daily use.

The idea of forming an official charity for children became a priority in my mind. The alarming conditions of sick and malnourished children urgently required a more substantial and specific aid. In 1994 I became more determined to go ahead with this project and went to see

25

Sabah Mahmoud, a dear friend and a lawyer, who became the first Trustee to join me and who stayed the full course of the charity. I was also very happy and honoured to invite Professor Soad Tabaqchali to join the Board of Trustees. Soad was Professor of Medical Microbiology and Clinical Director at St Bartholomew Hospital College, London. She remained a Trustee at the charity for nearly three years before resigning in 1998. With the three of us involved, MAIC was registered as a British charity in November 1994, with registration number 1044222. We started work in January 1995.

Chapter 2
United Nations Sanctions
Imposed on Iraq, 1990–2003

The 1990s were considered as the "sanctions decade", in light of the United Nations' (UN) extensive utilization of sanctions during that turbulent period. Before the 1990s, the UN had adopted sanctions only twice: against South Rhodesia in 1966, and against South Africa in 1977. However, since 1990, the UN and other regional organizations have also used sanctions against Iraq, Rwanda, Somalia, Liberia and Haiti, among other nations.[1]

Sanctions are perceived as "instruments of international politics". The UN imposes sanctions by resolutions adopted by the UN Security Council against a specific state. Sanctions are used as a forceful measure to compel a state to desist from engaging in acts violating international law.[2] The Council usually directs its sanctions operations through special sanctions committees.

---

[1] Garfield, Richard. 'The Silent Deadly Remedy: In the New World Order, Economic Sanctions May Leave No Dead Soldier, Just Civilian Casualties', Forum for Applied Research and Public Policy, 1999.

[2] Joyce, Christopher. 'United Nations Sanctions After Iraq: Looking Back to See Ahead', *Chicago Journal of International Law*, 2003.

UN Security Council Resolutions and Review Resolution SCR 661

In response to Iraq's invasion of Kuwait, the Security Council adopted, on 6 August 1990, Resolution 661 under Chapter Seven of the UN Charter. The resolution strictly prohibited all imports and exports in association with Iraq with the exception of medical supplies in humanitarian circumstances.[3]

The ultimate objectives of such restrictive economic measures were to achieve:

- the withdrawal of Iraqi troops from Kuwait;
- payment of war reparations to Kuwait;
- an end to human-rights violations; and
- the location and subsequent eradication of any weapons of mass destruction.[4]

The UN used Resolution 661 as a political tool to pressurise Saddam Hussein and his government to comply with the above stated objectives. Sadly, the Resolution had as well a disastrous effect on the Iraqi population. It caused over a million deaths, and millions more suffered from malnutrition. History had shown the devastating consequences of these harsh polices.

Never before had a country faced such prolonged economic stagnation; billions of dollars were lost in revenues from prohibited oil exports; there was a huge drop in industrial output and an enormous rise in inflation; and per capita income plummeted to levels equivalent to those found in the poorest countries.[5]

Above all, the most critical issue was human survival. The people of Iraq have had the most at stake, having suffered the consequences of impoverishment and malnutrition due to one

---

[3] UN Security Council 2933 Meeting 'Resolution 661(1990) The Situation Between Iraq and Kuwait'.

[4] Mazaheri, Nimah. 'Iraq and Domestic Political Effects of Economic Sanctions', *The Middle East Journal*, 2010.

[5] Garfield, 1999.

of the harshest economic blockades in history.[6] Chapter 5 looks more extensively at the harm caused by the excessive use of sanctions, especially on the health sector and particularly on children.

The period between 1990 and 1995 was fuelled by worldwide condemnation of the sanction regime. Hundreds of thousands of people demonstrated in the streets to protest against the sanctions. International humanitarian organizations, media and human-rights advocates published reports and showed documentaries about and pictures of suffering Iraqis. Delegates from the UN agencies, UNICEF, the World Health Organization (WHO), the Food and Agricultural Organization (FAO) and other organizations visited Iraq and published their alarming statistics.

A UNICEF report of 30 April 1998 states that malnutrition was not a public health problem in Iraq before the sanctions. The problem became evident during 1991 and sharply increased throughout the sanction years. In their comparative report for children under five between 1991 and 1996, children with underweight malnutrition increased from 9 per cent to 26 per cent, while chronic malnutrition (stunting) increased from 18 per cent to 31 per cent and malnutrition with wasting (acute malnutrition) increased from 3 per cent to 11 per cent. By 1997; it was estimated that about one million children under five were (chronically) malnourished.[7]

A survey conducted by FAO/WFP/WHO found that two million children were registered in 1998 as suffering from deficiencies in protein-, calorie- and vitamin-related malnutrition.[8] According to a FAO study, more than 560,000 Iraqi children died from hunger and disease between 1990 and

---

[6] Cortight, David, and Lopez, A. 'Are Sanctions Just? Problematic Case of Iraq', *Journal of International Affairs*, 1999.

[7] UNICEF Report. 'Situation Analysis of Children and Women in Iraq', UNICEF, 30 April 1998.

[8] Dr Kreisel, W. Executive Director of WHO Office 'Health Situation in Iraq', Brussels, 26 February 2001.

1995[9] and of course there were further deaths as sanctions continued.

Many of the thousands of excess deaths could have been prevented had basic medications been available. Treatments for simple diseases, such as diarrhoea and respiratory infections, were unavailable. Also, other essential items were in short supply, such as surgical items i.e. cannulas, blood bags, baby milk etc. Those shortages and others exacerbated further the poor health of children.

UN Security Council Resolution 986, "Oil-for-Food Programme" (OFFP)

Under the pressure of world opinion against the sanctions on Iraq, the Security Council reviewed its regime of sanctions and introduced, with the agreement of the Iraqi government, the "Oil-for-Food Programme". It was 'a temporary measure to provide for the humanitarian needs of the Iraqi people'. Although Resolution 986 was adopted in April 1995, it was implemented in December 1996. The first shipment of food sent by the programme arrived in March 1997.[10]

The programme allowed Iraq to sell up to two billion dollars' worth of oil over a period of six months and to use the oil proceeds for the purchase of humanitarian goods. In April 1998 the ceiling on oil exports was raised to $5,265 billion every six months. The ceiling was later lifted in 1999.[11]

The UN initially determined that 53 per cent of oil revenue would be allocated to the humanitarian programme in the areas under the control of the Iraqi government: 30 per cent would go to pay for compensation claims arising out of the Gulf War; 13 per cent would go to the UN programme in the Kurdish regions of North Iraq, and the remainder would be spent on further administrative costs of the UN. Organization of the programme was undertaken in six-months "phases", where every six months the Iraqi government

---

[9] Garfield, 1999.

[10] United Nations Office of the Iraq Programme. 'Oil-for-Food' home page, 4 November 2003, www.un.org/Depts/oip/

[11] Ibid.

presented a proposal of import contracts to be examined which, if judged adequate, would be approved by the UN Sanctions Committee.[12]

The programme was never intended to act as a substitute for the independent functioning of the Iraqi economy. The Security Council Resolution 986 itself refers to the programme as a 'temporary measure' to alleviate some of the hardship facing the population.[13]

The process of "Oil-for-Food Programme" administration proved 'incredibly burdensome' for members of the Iraq Sanctions Committee (drawn from the Security Council membership as a whole), who were required to authorize purchases and payments.[14] It also stretched the capacity of the UN secretariat, especially because of the illogical nature of some of the tasks required, which were beyond its competence.

However, the sale of oil through the programme, together with the funds from oil illegally smuggled out of Iraq barely kept the country functioning. Food and essential items were distributed through a rationing system which had existed before 1990. The ration, set before the implementation of Resolution 986, provided 1,275 calories per person, way below its pre-1990 level. Such a low level of calorie intake is seen only in the world's poorest countries.[15] According to FAO, widespread starvation was prevented by the rationing system, which provided minimum quantities of food to the population.[16]

During the late 1990s, slight improvements were recognized. Even with the improvements, the total number of

---

[12] Campaign Against Sanctions on Iraq (CASI), 8 March 2011.

[13] United Nations Office, 2000.

[14] Doxey, Margaret. 'Reflections on the Sanctions Decade of Beyond', *International Journal*, 2009.

[15] Alnasrawi, Abbas. *Iraq's Burdens: Oil, Sanctions and Underdevelopment,* Westport, CT: Greenwood Press, 2002.

[16] Food and Agriculture Organisation of the United Nations, Joint FAO/WEP Mission to Iraq. 'Malnutrition is Still Widespread', 16 October 1997.

chronically malnourished people remained very high. In the "Assessment of the Food and Nutrition Situation in Iraq", carried out by FAO/WFP/WHO for May–June 2000, it was confirmed that 800,000 children under five suffered from chronic malnutrition.[17]

Worldwide criticism against sanctions mounted throughout the 1990s. During this period, two of the UN Coordinators in Iraq, Denis Halliday and Hans Von Sponeck, resigned their posts in 1998 and 1999 respectively, in protest against the alarming consequences of sanctions. In an interview on 10 December 1998, Denis Halliday stated that over 6,000 Iraqi children were dying every month.

The "Oil-for-Food Programme" continued until the start of the second Gulf War on 19 March 2003. Moreover, during the period prior to the war, new strategies for applying UN sanctions were devised.

From December 2000 to February 2001, professed "fast track" lists were drawn up that speeded up the approval process for certain items used for housing, education, electricity, water and sanitation. Other strategies were also under study.

Security Council Resolution 1382: "Smart Sanctions"

The United States and United Kingdom introduced in 2001 a package of proposals under the label of "Smart Sanctions".[18] The term was used to refer to military-related items, as opposed to comprehensive economic sanctions.[19]

After some resistance at the Security Council, Resolution 1382 was adopted in November 2001. It drew up a long list of forbidden items labelled as 'dual use', as well as a draft recommendation for an even longer list.[20] Ultimately, the situation grew more complex and created more obstacles in its implementation.

---

[17] Kreisel, 2001.
[18] CASI, 2011.
[19] Joyce, 2003.
[20] *Ibid.*

Security Council Resolution 1472

The Security Council adopted Resolution 1472 following the end of the second Gulf War on 28 March 2003. The resolution adjusted the "Oil-for-Food Programme" to facilitate and speed up the delivery and receipt of goods for humanitarian needs.[21]

Security Council Resolution 1483

The Security Council lifted sanctions on Iraq on 22 May 2003 by adopting Resolution 1483. It authorized the Secretary General to appoint a Special Representative to work with the "Coalition Provisional Authority", which represented the occupying powers. The function of the representative was to transfer responsibility and terminate the "Oil-for-Food Programme" within six months. The programme came to an end on 21 November 2003.[22]

---

[21] United Nations Office, 2003.
[22] *Ibid.*

Chapter 3
Medical Aid for Iraqi Children (MAIC), 1995–2009

Although relatively short-lived, Medical Aid for Iraqi Children (MAIC), founded in 1995, provided crucial aid to many paediatric hospitals in Iraq during one of the most challenging periods of the country's modern history.

Throughout this turbulent period, MAIC's members worked relentlessly to provide medical supplies to children's hospitals in the centre, north and south of Iraq. Together, we faced many obstacles and challenges, yet the passion for the rightness of the cause empowered us to continue. A special salute goes to the marvellous Iraqi doctors who were in Iraq at the time. Their professionalism, coordination and courage were unforgettable and we also owe a great deal to thousands of wonderful people from different countries and religions, who constituted the lifeline of the charity through their continued donations and support.

Operating MAIC from 1995 onwards was a great challenge. Iraq was already suffering from crippling UN sanctions following Security Council Resolution 661, which had been imposed on the country in August 1990. Moreover, Iraq had been devastated by two wars, the Iran–Iraq war of 1980–1988 and the first Gulf War, which began in 1991. The wars destroyed its institutions, its vital utilities and its means of communication. Iraq was in a state of total isolation. At that time any gesture, even providing humanitarian aid to children, was regarded with suspicion by the West.

MAIC's first Board of Governors was appointed by its three Trustees, Professor Soad Tabaqchali, Sabah Mahmoud and myself and included, apart from the Trustees, seven other members in London. The Board appointed a Medical Team in Iraq of four members, a Jordanian Liaison Committee of seven members and an Honorary Committee of ten members (see Appendix 2).

We started work in 1995, once the registration of the charity was completed and we had opened a bank account and made a small initial donation. We held charity meetings for the first couple of years and conducted our work from my home and from Sabah's office.

Over the next few years, MAIC expanded. We moved to an official charity office in 1998 with just one paid secretary, to keep our costs to a minimum. The members increased in number, reaching a total of forty-seven by the time the charity ceased operation (see Appendix 3). The enthusiasm and team-oriented spirit of all our members, whether in London, Baghdad or Jordan, were the driving force behind achieving our mission and saving the lives of thousands of children. Soon, MAIC changed from a small home-based charity to one that was internationally recognised, with a large number of supporters.

During the sanction years, our medical aid reached twenty-six hospitals throughout Iraq, at a time when very little aid was filtering in. The process of taking supplies into Iraq during this period required painstaking procedures. In order to obtain approvals from the UN Security Council Sanctions Committee in New York and receive export licences from the Department of Trade and Industry DTI in London, we had to deal with some extremely difficult bureaucratic bodies.

Transportation of medical supplies to Iraq was another hurdle. Flights into and out of Iraq were not allowed under the UN sanctions. Therefore, supplies had to be shipped by sea from the UK to Aqaba in Jordan. Once the supplies arrived in Aqaba, MAIC's Jordanian Liaison Committee, headed by Dr Junaid Mahmoud, arranged its clearance from Jordanian customs and loaded the supplies onto trucks, to be transported to Baghdad. The hazardous land journey used to take around sixteen hours. As a safety measure, and to ensure clearance of the supplies at border checkpoints and their safe delivery to the storage facility at the Medical City in Baghdad, Hani Salim, a reliable male nurse, was employed to accompany the supplies. We used his services for a few years.

In Baghdad, MAIC's Medical Team, headed by Dr Khalid Al Obaydi, took delivery of the supplies and arranged their storage at the Medical City storage facility. The pre-packed samples of medicines, which were usually included with the supplies, were sent by the team doctors to the Central Health Laboratory to be analysed and approved. Once approved, MAIC's Medical Team arranged the distribution of the supplies to the assigned hospitals according to the labels which had been attached to the boxes in the warehouse in London prior to their shipment.

Our aid continued from 1995 throughout the second Gulf War in 2003 and for six years after that, until the closure of the charity in 2009. During the fourteen years we were in operation, we raised £3.7 million from fundraising events, donations and sponsorship from foundations, cooperates and individuals. The cost of running the charity was kept to a minimum. MAIC's aid to paediatric hospitals totalled £3.5 million worth of medical supplies. It included two complete three-bed paediatric intensive care units, diagnostic equipment, incubators and hundreds of wheelchairs and crutches. The supplies also included surgical items, a variety of medicines, especially anti-cancer drugs and third-generation antibiotics, as well as vitamins and minerals. We estimate that around 350,000 children benefited from our aid.

MAIC also sponsored nine Iraqi doctors in short training programmes at UK hospitals between 2005 and 2008. The training was offered free by the UK hospitals while MAIC paid for their travelling and living expenses.

Although our medical aid increased in quantity and value after the second Gulf War in 2003, sadly it was limited to fewer hospitals. Up until the 2003 war, MAIC provided aid to a total of twenty-six hospitals. Many of them received aid once or twice a year (see Appendix 4). Later, a few more hospitals were added to the list, but many more dropped off it, due to new obstacles.

Sadly, after March 2003, the number of hospitals receiving aid was significantly reduced. Many factors contributed to this drop, including:

→ The lack of security made some areas very dangerous to reach. Moreover, the cost of employing security guards to accompany the supplies became exorbitant, which made the distribution to some hospitals impossible.

→ The new law issued by the Iraqi government after 2003 restricted hospitals from receiving aid directly from charities. Some hospitals were afraid to accept medical supplies directly from us even though they were in extreme need of aid.

The above factors together with the following developments did influence our decision later on to close the charity:

• The requirement of an Import Licence from the Iraqi government to take any goods into Iraq, even if they were donated by a charity, complicated matters. Goods that did not have an Import Licence were subjected to custom duty. We had to pay US $3,000 in custom duty on one of our last medical consignments as it crossed the Iraqi border in 2009.

• The frequently change of hospital directors made communications and follow-up with them very difficult, especially because some of them were also incompetent.

• The fact that some of the Trustees were retiring and we were unable to find new Trustees with the required commitment to take over and deal with those complicated issues efficiently.

After painstaking consideration of the future of MAIC, a decision was sadly made on 21 May 2009 at the Trustees Board meeting attended by: Hani Dajani, Fatima Khazaal, Robert Mabro, Sabah Mahmoud, Doris Riachi and myself to wind up the charity on 31 July 2009.

MAIC ceased its operations on 24 July 2009 after shipping its last medical consignment, which was delivered later, in September and October, to four hospitals, two in Baghdad: the Children's Welfare Teaching Hospital and the Central Paediatric Teaching Hospital, and two in Basrah: the Basrah Teaching Hospital and the Basrah Prosthetic Centre.

The remaining funds after paying all expenses were distributed to three charities in London – the Iraqi Orphan Foundation (£2,000), Shams Fund (£12,658) and Great Ormond Street Children's Hospital (£5,000).

MAIC was one of the very few charities, if not the only one, which was successful in making a tangible difference to the medical needs of paediatric hospitals in Iraq. Unlike other larger international aid organisations which provided basic medical supplies, MAIC responded to the urgent and specific requirements of the hospitals, which were directly advised by its network of doctors who worked at the hospitals.

A group photo of MAIC's Trustees, Board of Governors and some
of the Honorary Members at the inauguration of the Charity.
Mayfair Hotel, London, 6 May 1995.

Professor Soad Tabaqchali and Sabah Mahmoud, members of
MAIC's Trustees, inspecting the Charity's consignment at
Commercial Transport International UK. London, 1995.

Hani Dajani, a MAIC Trustee, and May Al-Daftari inspecting
MAIC's medical consignment before shipment. London, 1999.

Chapter 4

Dealing with Sanction Regulations in Sending Medical Supplies to Iraq and Examples Encountered by MAIC

Following Resolution 661, which imposed sanctions on Iraq on 6 August 1990, the UN issued an application form to be completed by missions or international organizations intending to ship goods to Iraq. A sample of a UN Application form and a Guidance Note by the British Department of Trade and Industry (DTI) have been reproduced (see Appendix 5).

Filling in the form was one of the most complicated and time-consuming processes our charity had to undertake. It required tedious details: a description of each item, as well as a quantification of the unit of measurement, the quantity, the type of packaging used, how many items were included per package, the unit value and the total value.

Once each form was completed, we sent it to the DTI in London for processing. It remained with the DTI for four to six weeks, sometimes even more, before they had to send it to the UN Mission in New York. During this period the DTI often sent us queries, such as asking for the chemical components of certain medicines, or for extra clarification on the units of measurement, or on technical specifications or the type of use for certain pieces of medical equipment.

Once the form was cleared from the DTI departments and received by the UN Mission in New York, it was presented to the UN Security Council Sanctions Committee. The Form remained with the Committee for a couple of weeks, where it was evaluated and examined. On approval, the UN letter of authorization was issued and sent to the DTI in London to issue the export licence (see Appendix 6 and Appendix 7). This last phase of issuing the export license usually took a few weeks to process. The whole operation, from the time we submitted the form to the DTI to the day we received the export license from the DTI took between six and nine months.

Apart from the above difficulties, MAIC was faced with further problems due to the strict nature of the sanctions system and its inability to accommodate for technical changes to name of products or their descriptions. On certain occasions we were faced by unhelpful personnel who tried to block an item which had already a UN approval.

Examples of Problems Encountered by MAIC:

$\rightarrow$ **Vickers Infant Incubators**

In 1995, we were advised to send two incubators to the Ibn Baladi Paediatric Hospital in Baghdad. The hospital's many incubators were dilapidated and many were hardly functioning. Most of the newborns were extremely underweight, and were struggling for their lives without functioning incubators. Doctors at the neonatal wards were desperate to have incubators – it was a priority on their list of urgent medical needs.

Prior to 1990, Iraq used to import Vickers incubators from the United States. The medical staff at the neonatal wards were familiar with this brand and knew how to operate it. We therefore included in the UN Application Form two Vickers infant incubators (C286 model), along with a list of medical supplies earmarked for the Ibn Baladi Paediatric Hospital.

After submitting the form and waiting for a few months between the processing at the DTI and the evaluation at the UN Sanctions Committee, we received the UN authorization.

However, subsequent to ordering the two Vickers incubators from the supplier, International Health Services Limited ECHO, we received on 17 October 1995 a letter from

ECHO addressed to Professor Tabaqchali, MAIC Trustee, informing the charity that the US Treasury (the Office of Foreign Assets Control OFAC) had blocked the processing of the license for the incubators. Also, death threats were received by workers at Vickers (see Appendix 8).

The supplier, ECHO, advised us to wait for a while as a Vickers UK representative was travelling to the US and would try to sort out the matter. After further communications, we were advised on 12 December 1995 to cancel the two incubators and proceed with sending the rest of the medical supplies before the UN authorization document expired. It was difficult for those of us who worked at the charity to understand the action of the US Treasury, which seemed inhumane because it prevented doctors from saving the lives of newborns with desperately needed incubators.

Eventually, the problem of the incubators was resolved by providing them through another representative in London. After this incident, we started buying incubators from the manufacturer Dragger in Germany until 2000, when Iraq started importing Alom incubators from Japan. Following the implementation of the Resolution 986 "Oil-for-Food Programme", the Iraqi government was allowed to sell limited amounts of oil and import medical supplies and food conditional to UN approval.

→ **Three Heart Monitors and a Central Working Station**

After the success of donating a three-bed intensive care unit ICU from Siemens, Germany, to the Al Mansour Paediatric Teaching Hospital in Baghdad, we decided to send another, similar, ICU to the Central Paediatric Teaching Hospital in Baghdad, Al Tifl Al Markazi. In April 2000, we submitted an application to the DTI listing the components of the ICU to go through the usual process of authorisation. A few months later, some of the components were approved, but the three essential heart monitors and a central working station, were rejected by the US Treasury. Although the equipment was German-made, some parts made in the US were included. We had to submit another application in January 2001, which caused an unnecessarily long delay before the ICU was operational.

→ **Blood Glucose Monitoring**

Following our application for a "Glucose Meter for Diabetic Patients" in September 2000, and long delays for the authorisation, the model was discontinued. It was replaced by another equivalent model called 'Blood Glucose Monitoring'. The change of the model name created a problem of documentation for the licence. The lack of flexibility for a simple change in specification prevented us from sending this urgently needed equipment with the rest of the supplies and necessitated another application and a delay of several months.

→ **Sutures**

Another example of lack of flexibility occurred when we needed to replace a box of sutures with another box containing sutures of a smaller size. We used to send paediatric hospitals boxes of differently sized sutures to be used in surgery. Suture sizes were based on what was commonly used at British paediatric hospitals. Doctors at the Iraqi hospitals advised us of their urgent need to have thinner sutures for surgeries to be carried out on babies and newborns as the children they were treating were extremely small and underweight. Unfortunately, when we wrote to the DTI asking for permission to replace a box of sutures, which already had the approval of the UN, with another box containing thinner sutures, it was not possible. We could not include the thinner sutures with the rest of the consignment due to the delay in acquiring a special permission for the exchange before the expiry date of the UN licence. The rigidity of the system resulted in a further delay of several months during which many babies could have had surgeries and been saved. We had to fill in another application and wait a few more months to send an urgently needed box of sutures which could have helped many babies if they had been sent in time.

The charity continued to face bureaucratic problems and delays until 22 May 2003 when the UN sanctions were removed.

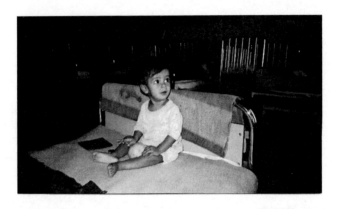

A sixteen-month-old boy suffering from a chest infection at Ibn Baladi Paediatric Hospital. Baghdad, 7 October 1998.

May Al-Daftari and Dr Khalid Al Obaydi visiting the three-bed Intensive Care Unit for children, donated by MAIC to Al Mansour Paediatric Teaching Hospital. In the photo as well is Dr Mahmoud Maki, director of the hospital, September 2000.

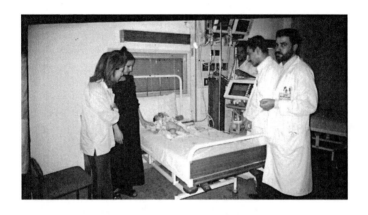

The children's ICU, which was donated by MAIC to the hospital,
is being used by a four-month-old baby girl, September 2000.

Chapter 5
Health Conditions in Iraq and the Role of Iraqi Doctors

In order to evaluate fully the health conditions in Iraq, it is imperative to compare health indicators prior to and after 1990, when UN sanctions were imposed. I will also add our charity's observations made during my visits to health centres between 1996 and 2001 and comments made by other members of the charity as well as quotes taken from papers given at MAIC's "Forum on Health of Children in Iraq" held in London on 3 March 2005. It is also vital to review the significant role played by MAIC's team of doctors in Iraq, to further understand how they coped with the dire health conditions which prevailed during the sanction years in hospitals.

Overview Prior to 1990

Whatever were the flaws with Saddam Hussein's violent rule of Iraq and his human rights violations, historians and political commentators would agree that Iraq was viewed in the 1980s as a country belonging to a middle-income group of countries, with a GDP per capita of USD 2,800.[23] According to a UN report, Iraq was described in the mid-1980s as a state that had an elaborate health-care system, a modern telecommunication network, twenty-four electrical power-generating systems and sophisticated water-treatment

---

[23] Dr Kreisel, W. Executive Director WHO Office of the European Union, 'Health Situation in Iraq', Brussels, 26 February 2001.

plants.[24] Iraq also had an effective sewage-treatment system which largely reduced the threat of a communicable diseases outbreak.

The Medical University in Iraq that was established in 1927 was considered one of the leading universities in the Middle East. Many of its graduates acquired worldwide reputations and became very successful doctors in UK and United States hospitals. Up to 1990, medical standards in Iraq were considered the best in the Middle East. Iraq had a national Compulsory Education Law and was honoured by UNESCO for its active promotion of education.[25]

In 1981, the Ministry of Health, in its drive to offer free health care to Iraq's rural and urban citizens, set up 194 public hospitals, 1,168 primary health-care centres and 242 mobile health centres for rural areas.[26] Before 1990, there were also 148 functioning ambulances. Ambulances and emergency services were all well developed and benefited from a properly maintained network of roads and telecommunications.[27] In 1989, the Iraqi Ministry of Health spent more than US $500 million on drugs and medical supplies.[28]

An important measure by which to evaluate children's health is the mortality rates for both infants and children under five. A UNICEF survey published in 1999 shows that between 1984 and 1989, the mortality rates in Iraq were 56 deaths per 1,000 live births and 47 deaths per 1,000 under-fives.[29] Moreover, there was an outstanding improvement in the year 1988–1989 in the rate of childhood immunizations

---

[24] UN Report, October 1991.
[25] UNICEF Report. 'Situation Analysis: Children and Women in Iraq', 30 April 1998.
[26] Stephen. 'Primary Health Care in the Arab World', Somerset House UK, 1992.
[27] Kreisel, 2001.
[28] UNICEF, 1998.
[29] UNICEF. 'Child and Maternal Survey', 12 August 1999.

against tuberculosis, diphtheria, pertussis, tetanus, polio and measles.[30]

Overview After 1990

The comprehensive sanctions in 1990, combined with the effect of the first Gulf War, destroyed the country's vital utilities and health institutions. They also prevented Iraq from importing spare parts for repairs, bringing about catastrophic health hazards. The destruction of the sewage system and water plants during the war resulted in a lack of safe potable water and contaminated the sanitary system. This led to the spread of infections and waterborne diseases; previously eradicated diseases, such as malaria, typhoid, cholera and typhus, reappeared. Moreover, medicines, vaccines and the childhood immunisation programme were practically unavailable, thus making treatment impossible for a large spectrum of diseases.

Between 1990 and 1995, the childhood immunisation programme, which is the right of every child in the world, was severely disrupted. As well as shortage of vaccines, the problem was exacerbated by erratic electrical supplies, which compromised the cold-storage facilities in medical centres. Children were no longer protected against preventable diseases such as measles, mumps, diphtheria, polio, tetanus, whooping-cough and meningitis. The situation became more critical, with millions of children remaining unprotected. As the pressure from international health institutions increased, immunisation against polio was eventually provided to children in 2000 and 2001.

Following the adoption of sanctions on Iraq in 1990, inflation rocketed and GDP per capita was reduced to its lowest levels, dropping from around USD 1,500 to USD 600.

---

[30] UNICEF Report. 'The State of the World's Children', Oxford University Press, 1991.

The salary of a public worker averaged between USD3 and USD5 per month.[31]

By 1995, the UN Department of Humanitarian Affairs estimated that around four million Iraqis lived in extreme poverty. The purchasing power of the Iraqi currency, the dinar, was reduced from USD3:1dinar in 1990 (before the sanctions) to around USD1:1,500 dinars in 1997.[32]

As a result of all these factors, especially the absence of potable water, the unavailability of spare parts to repair vital utilities, the spread of diseases and the scarcity of medical supplies, the collapse of the economy and the sharp drop in the value of the dinar, led to a critical situation of reduced nutrition affecting the majority of Iraqis.

Malnutrition, which had not existed before the sanctions, now became a major health problem. By 1997, according to a joint FAO/WEP mission to Iraq, the team found that, even after the introduction of the "Oil-for-Food Programme", malnutrition was still a major problem in Iraq. Marasmus and Kwashiorkor, well-known malnutrition diseases, (usually observed in famine-like countries) were reported by the team to be spreading wildly.[33] Another report by FAO/WFP/WHO published in 2000, confirmed that about 800,000 children under five were chronically malnourished. It also stated that anaemia, rickets and vitamin D deficiency prevailed among schoolchildren.[34] In an earlier report, the World Food Programme WFP stated that 23 percent of Iraqi children below the age of five suffered from malnutrition. The report also attributed 39 percent of child mortality to malnutrition.[35]

---

[31] Arya, Neil, and Zurbrigg, Sheila. 'Operation Infinite: Impact of Sanctions and Prospective War on the People of Iraq', *Canadian Journal of Public Health*, 2003.

[32] UNICEF, 1998.

[33] Food and Agricultural Organization of the United Nations: FAO/WFP Assessment Mission in Iraq, June–July Special Report on 3 October 1997.

[34] FAO/WFP/WHO. 'Assessment of Food and Nutrition Situation in Iraq', May–June 2000.

[35] World Food Programme (WFP), June 1995.

The spread of cancers, especially leukaemia, among children was another major problem. There was also a sharp rise in the number of children with birth deformities.

Comparing both mortality rates for infants and under-fives in 1994–1999 with rates prior to 1990, show a significant rise: 108 deaths per 1,000 live births and 131 deaths per 1,000 for the under-fives.[36]

Moreover, the Food and Agriculture Organisation (FAO), estimates that 560,000 children died between 1990 and 1995 from hunger and disease.[37] Another survey by FAO in 1995 showed that 28 percent of children had stunted growth, 29 percent were underweight and 12 percent showed signs of wasting. Most of those children would not be able to catch up with their potential intellectual and physical growth.

The second Gulf War, which started on 19 March 2003, brought about new complications to the life of this ailing population. The rise in violence and lack of security that followed the war, led to the death of scores of people and inflicted crippling injuries, with children being the main victims. It also increased the already high level of trauma among them. Anxiety and depression became serious decapitating diseases that affected thousands of children; many of them suffered from Post Traumatic Disorder, a psychological illness new to most Iraqi doctors, who were not familiar with its treatment at that time.

The escalation of violence also resulted in "brain drain" among doctors and academics. Doctors also became victims of attacks and kidnapping for ransom. Hundreds of doctors and nurses were kidnapped and some were killed or injured. Dr Abdul Karim Alobedy MD, the Chair of the Iraqi Association for Child Mental Health, in his talk "The Plight of Academics in Iraq" at University College, London in 2006, referred to the UNHCR report of October 2005, which showed that more than 106 doctors, 164 nurses and 142 non-medical staff had been killed (see Appendix 9).

---

[36] UNICEF, 1999.

[37] Food and Agricultural Organization of the United Nations, 1997.

Education, an important sector for children and youth, was substantially degraded. Schools were dilapidated. Basic facilities such as safe sanitation, potable water and electricity were absent. Classrooms were damp with leaking ceilings, broken windows and shattered doors. Blackboards, chalks, paper (which had been designated as 'non-essential' by the Sanctions Committee), together with pencils and teaching aids, were all scarce.[38] Investment in education under the four phases of the "Oil-for-Food Programme" averaged $23m a year, compared to the $230m allocated in the mid-1980s.[39]

Observations by MAIC Members

First Impressions Following My Visit in February 1996

On 27 January 1996 I travelled to Baghdad by road to see my ailing mother and to visit paediatric hospitals, some of which had already received medical supplies from MAIC's first medical shipment, delivered in August and September 1995. The value of the shipment exceeded £50,000 and was delivered to four hospitals: the Al Mansour Paediatric Teaching Hospital, the Central Paediatric Teaching Hospital (Al Tifl Al Markazi), the Basrah Paediatric Hospital and the Mosul Paediatric Teaching Hospital.

Although it was a gruelling journey of sixteen hours along dreary desert roads, I nonetheless felt very positive. The journey brought many childhood memories. I arrived at my sister's house at night. I cannot describe the expression on my mother's face as I entered her room. My sister had not told her that I was coming. It was a total surprise for her and an intense emotional moment for all of us; it was indeed a much-longed-for family reunion after years of separation.

The next morning, I started unpacking and my nephew Shamil, who was in his early twenties at the time, was sitting on the sofa watching me. I put aside a bag filled with sweets and mini chocolate bars. Shamil stared at the bag and asked

---

[38] UNICEF, 1998.

[39] UNICEF Emergency Programmes Iraq Donor Update, 1, 'Emergency Overview and Recent Developments', 8 August 2000.

me what they were for. I said innocently that I would distribute them to the sick children during my visits to the hospitals. He turned to me and asked if I realised the value of each mini bar. He said that each would be worth 4,000 to 5,000 dinars if it was found in the black market. He continued to say that each bar was worth the equivalent of a month's salary for a doctor. His shocking remarks were my first encounter with the grave reality of what Iraqis were going through, evidence of the sharp drop in the value of their currency and in their living standards. After the 1991 Gulf War, the majority of Iraqis were left unemployed, each household barely living on a monthly income of less than USD 5.

A few days later, I visited, with my brother-in-law, Dr Ihssan Al Bahrani, four of the largest paediatric hospitals in Baghdad: Al Mansour Paediatric Teaching Hospital, the Central Paediatric Teaching Hospital (Al Tifal Al Merkazi), Ibn Baladi Obstetric Hospital and Karama Hospital.

It was a heart-breaking experience, seeing children in pain and in dire conditions, sharing beds with soiled mattresses with no sheets or blankets in the cold January weather. Wards were flooded with sewage water seeping from lavatories due to lack of chlorine and other dissolving chemicals. The UN Sanctions Committee required a special import licence for those items as they were considered of "duel use". Babies were lying in non-functioning incubators due to the absence of new incubators and of spare parts to repair the old ones.

Doctors were desperate to help these children and frustrated at the scarcity of medicines and surgical items. They had to make hard decisions about how best to utilise the meagre medicines and the very few surgical items available to treat the large number of patients. Medicines in general, such as antibiotics, cancer drugs, vitamins and proteins were scarce, and even simple remedies such as decongestants, allergy drugs, prednisolone, hydrocortisone and saline were missing. Resident doctors told us that children with chest infections and diarrhoea suffered and some even died from the absence of simple treatment and dehydration. There were also acute shortages in simple surgical items. Doctors complained that the scarcity of syringes, cannulas and fluid drips made the administration of injectable drugs impossible.

An eight-year-old girl diagnosed with Leukaemia at the Cancer ward at the Central Paediatric Teaching Hospital. Baghdad, September 2000

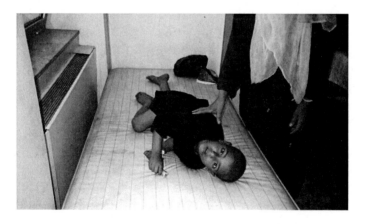

A young boy suffering from leukaemia and depression at Al Mansour Paediatric Teaching Hospital. October 1998.

As we walked through the wards, we saw children queuing for the same pack of drip and using the same cannula and syringe, and others sharing the same nebulizer. There was one mask adaptor at each ward which was used by groups of children, each child using it for five minutes.

We also saw children suffering from severe malnutrition diseases, acute anaemia, septicaemia and thalassemia. At the cancer ward, children had different types of malignancy and a large number of them had leukaemia. These children and their parents gazed at the passers-by and pleaded for help. I felt so helpless as I tried to comfort some of the parents and promised to send the drugs that were needed for their sick child, while silently and agonisingly wondering whether they could be delivered in time to treat their child.

During my visit to the neonatal ward at Ibn Baladi Obstetric, I saw babies lying in non-functional incubators and mothers struggling to feed their babies. Milk was another grave problem. After the bombing that destroyed the milk factory during the first Gulf War in 1991, there was no milk-producing factory left in Iraq. Mothers were weak and undernourished and hardly had any milk to feed their underweight babies. Formula milk was unavailable, due to its unclear specification on the UN Sanctions Committee lists about whether milk was a food or a medicine item.

Anaesthetics were another important, yet very scarce item needed for surgery. They were also considered to be a dual-use item and so a special licence was required to import them. Even at the teaching hospitals, where most operations took place, they were unavailable. Some of the urgent operations were carried out under local analgesic drugs. Sutures, another basic item used in surgery, were also lacking. Doctors expressed their concern about having to delay surgery because of the unavailability of most of the required drugs and surgical items.

At the end of my visit I met with some of MAIC's team of doctors, which included Dr Ihsan, Al Bahrani, Dr Khalid Al Obaydi, Dr Hussein Malik and Dr Hussam Charmougli. We discussed the appalling conditions in hospitals and compiled long lists of their urgent needs.

When I wasn't visiting hospitals, I spent all my time at my beloved mother's bedside. I knew it was my last chance to be with her. She passed away two months after my return to London.

Since then I continued to go to Iraq until 2001 to visit hospitals, evaluate health conditions and find out about their urgent medical needs.

Comments by Other MAIC Members

Mr Khalid Al Obaydi, MD Consultant Surgeon at the Medical City, Baghdad

In his letter of 22 May 1997, Khalid reviewed the dire conditions in several paediatric hospitals. Conditions had worsened in some more than in others. He pointed to the problems: an overload of patients; poor sanitation; rapid deterioration of drains resulting in blockages; and non-functioning cooling systems due to unavailable spare parts. He also pointed to the increase in the number of children with chronic cases and malignancy (see Appendix 10).

Mr Hassan Al Haddad, MD Orthopaedic Surgeon and Traumatology

In his letter of 17 June 1997, Hassan emphasised the problems doctors and medical staff were facing at Iraqi hospitals, naming some, including the scarcity of medicines in general and the unavailability of anaesthetic drugs, blood units, blood-preserving containers, plates and screws for fractures, sutures, oxygen masks, laboratory instruments and machinery (see Appendix 11).

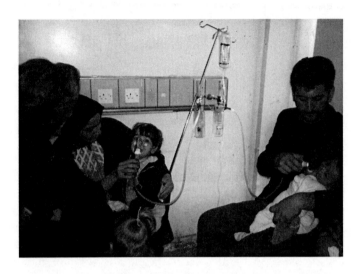

Children using scarce nebulizers, each allowed five minutes.
Central Paediatric Teaching Hospital. Baghdad, February 1996.

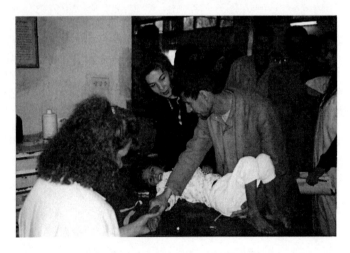

May Al-Daftari, Trustee and Chairman of MAIC, at the emergency
unit where a young girl was suffering from high fever and severe
diarrhoea. Al Karama Hospital. Baghdad, February 1996.

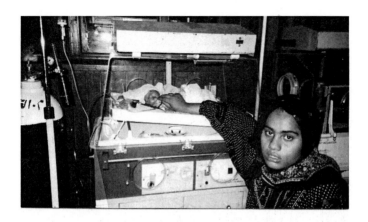

A mother holding an oxygen nasal tube to help her distressed new-born to breath in a non-functional incubator. Ibn Baladi Obstetric Hospital, Baghdad, February 1996.

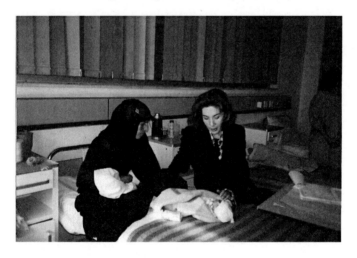

May Al-Daftari visiting a neonatal ward where babies were in urgent need of simple treatments which were scarce in most hospitals. Ibn Baladi Hospital, Baghdad, February 1996.

May Al-Daftari checking hospital records and receipts for MAIC's medical consignments sent to hospitals at Medical City storage facility. Medical City, Baghdad, 1998.

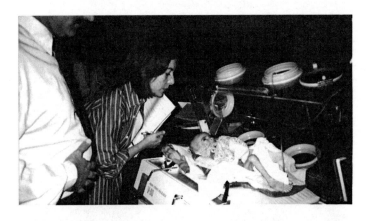

May Al-Daftari viewing a ten-month-old baby suffering from chronic diarrhoea and retarded growth. Al Mansour Paediatric Teaching Hospital, Baghdad, March 1998.

Dr Ihsan Al Bahrani, a Professor and Prominent Cardiologist

Ihsan in his letter stated that: 'Diagnostic equipment was either obsolete or in need of spare parts; as an example, out of the four CT scanners in Iraq, only one was functioning. Most laboratory equipment, renal dialysis units and sonographer machines were out of order. Also, the erratic supply of electricity and the frequent power cuts created major problems for hospitals and storage facilities; they interrupted the required refrigeration and cooling systems and other essential hospital services thus causing the wasting of scarce medicines.'

Dr Jawad Khadem Al Ali, Head of the Oncology Department at Basrah Hospital

Jawad cited statistics that he linked to exposure to DU: the rate of cancers had multiplied by ten since 1988; the death rate from cancers had multiplied by nineteen since 1988; congenital malformations in newborns had multiplied by seven since 1990; new and strange phenomena of cancers appeared such as cluster cancers in families and double and triple cancers among individuals. (Published in MAIC Newsletter, Autumn 2004.)

Dr Mazen Al Jadiry, Resident Oncologist at Al Mansour Paediatric Hospital, Baghdad

During my visit in 2000 to the cancer unit at Al Mansour Hospital, Mazen provided the following statistics from his records: between 1979 and 1991 there were 300 children registered at the unit. After this period, there was a sharp increase in cancer patients, with 1,119 children registered at the unit between 1991 and 2000. The number of children with cancers had almost quadrupled since the end of the first Gulf War. Leukaemia accounted for 70 percent of childhood cancer cases, followed by non-Hodgkin's lymphoma, Wilm's tumour (nephroblastoma) and neuroblastoma. (Published in MAIC Newsletter, Autumn 2000.)

In her essay "Iraq's Heath Care System: Hope or Despair?", Maya gives a concise review of health conditions in later years up to 2007. (Published in MAIC Newsletter, Autumn 2007; see Appendix 12.)

Forum on the Health of Children in Iraq

The forum was held by MAIC on 3 May 2005 at the Royal Geographical Society in London. The panel was moderated by the late Mr Robert Mabro CBE, MAIC Trustee. Experts on the panel were Professor William Yule, Director of the Child Traumatic Stress Clinic at Maudsley Hospital, London and Dr Penelope Brock, Consultant Paediatric Oncologist at Great Ormond Street Hospital, London. The speakers included three doctors from Iraq: Mr Hussein Malik, Paediatric Surgeon, Dr Ali Hameed Rashid, Paediatric Psychologist, Dr Jawad Khadem Al Ali, Oncologist and Ms Lindsay Hillsum, Channel 4 News International Editor. (Resume of the papers published in MAIC Newsletter, Autumn 2005; see Appendix 13.)

MAIC's Medical Team in Iraq

Members of the Medical Team in Iraq were appointed by the charity's Board of Governors. Over the years some members joined and others left as they fled Iraq during the period where doctors were targeted and kidnapped. In 1995 the team included Dr Khalid Al Obaydi, Dr Adel Al Rawi, Dr Omar Al Yaqubi and Dr Hussam Charmougli. Dr Ihsan Al Bahrani and Dr Hussein Malik joined in 1997 and 1998 respectively. By 2009 the team members were Dr Jawad Khadem Al Ali, Dr Adel Al Rawi, Dr Omar Al Yaqubi and Dr Mazin Al Jadiry. All the doctors were most supportive and gave their valuable advice whenever it was needed. However, in the following pages I will review the contribution of five doctors who were most active during the life of MAIC.

Dr Khalid Al Obaydi MD, Surgeon and Director General of Medical City, Baghdad

A few days after my arrival in Baghdad in January 1996, I went with my brother-in-law, Dr Ihsan Al Bahrani, to meet members of our Medical Team in Iraq whom the Trustees had previously appointed.

Our first visit was to see Dr Khalid Al Obaydi at the Medical City. Although I had already established contact with him through letters sent by hand and through difficult operator-conducted telephone calls, it was the first time I had seen Khalid face to face. I was little apprehensive at the start, expecting to see an authoritative person in charge of this large establishment, which comprises eleven hospitals. We met at his office at one of the hospitals, which was known at the time as Al Mansour Paediatric Teaching Hospital (the name was changed after 2003 to the Welfare Teaching Hospital).

Khalid's warm welcome, his soft-spoken manner and his words of appreciation for MAIC's aid were the start of nine years of professional cooperation. Ihsan knew Khalid well as he had been one of his students and he had recommended him to join the charity's Medical Team in Iraq.

During the one-hour meeting, I was able to comprehend a fraction of the vast problems the hospital was facing due to the effect of the UN sanctions regime which restricted and slowed down aid. I also realised the load of responsibilities Khalid was dealing with on a daily basis.

Prior to our meeting, Ihsan and I were seated in a waiting room crowded with children accompanied by their parents. I spoke to a few of the parents and heard their heart-breaking stories. Many of them came from faraway villages where medical care was nearly absent. Most of the children needed urgent surgery but had to wait their turn in a long queue.

During the meeting I inquired from Khalid about the treatment of those children and asked how soon they could have their surgery. He explained the difficulties the hospital was facing due to the lack of medicines, anaesthetics, surgical supplies etc. Each case needed to be reviewed and scheduled for surgery according to its urgency. Often a child had to wait months or years, depending on the availability of anaesthetics. Some operations were carried out with analgesic only. Sutures and cannulas were also missing, alongside other urgent necessities for surgery.

Throughout the meeting, nurses, doctors and hospital staff came in and out, presenting Khalid with different problems. To my surprise, one of the nurses asked him for a piece of soap for one of the wards. Khalid went and opened a cupboard, took a soap bar, cut it into three parts and gave her one part. The unavailability of this basic hygiene item was a stark reminder of the gravity of the situation and its effect on the health of Iraqis.

From 1995 and until 2004, Khalid was the core of our team of doctors in Iraq. He was professional, efficient and showed remarkable care for his patients. He regularly supplied MAIC with detailed lists of medicines, surgical items and equipment which were urgently needed by the paediatric hospitals in the north, centre and south of Iraq. He also sent us receipts once the medical supplies were received. His lengthy, detailed letters were very valuable to MAIC's Board members. His letters, apart from the general updates, included the licence from the Health Laboratory, which allows the use of medicines in hospitals. The letters also confirm the distribution of the supplies to the assigned hospitals with hospital receipts signed by the receiving staff. (Samples of his letters can be read in Appendix 14 and Appendix 15.)

During my later visits to Iraq, I kept meeting with Khalid and other doctors from MAIC's Medical Team. We toured the receiving hospitals, evaluated the use of MAIC's aid and took notes of their pressing medical needs. We also inspected equipment that had been donated by MAIC, such as incubators, blood analyser machines and the intensive care unit.

Khalid also arranged for me to go through the aid record for MAIC at Al Mansour Paediatric hospital. Our charity record was included in a record book that covers the aid given by different charities. I was very impressed by the details listed. Even during that period of hardship under sanctions, hospital staff kept orderly records of each charity's donations, listing the names of each medicine that had been donated as well as their quantities, the names of patients treated with it and the dates on which they were treated. The medical staff that I met did their best to keep up with international medical standards. I admired the dedication of the Iraqi doctors and their organisation of hospital records, even though they were living under tremendous pressure.

Once, I asked Khalid if hospitals would accept short-shelf-life medicines, as many pharmaceuticals were offering MAIC such medicines free of charge. He replied: 'It is easier to cope with the effects of sanctions than break the rules of medical standards that doctors in Iraq were practicing for over half a century.' Throughout the fourteen years of our operation, we made sure that all medicines donated to Iraq had a shelf life of at least one to two years.

Unfortunately, those standards and medical ethics were shattered after the second Gulf War in 2003 and thirteen years of sanctions, due to many factors:

→ The damage done to Iraq's infrastructure and its vital utilities, which had a devastating effect on the health system.
→ The looting of hospitals by mobs immediately after the second Gulf War and the kidnapping of doctors, many of whom were killed.
→ The replacement of experienced doctors with others, following the regime change, based in many cases on their political and religious affiliations, rather than their merits.

Sadly, in 2003 Khalid was replaced. After a few months he left with his family for Abu Dhabi. No longer having Khalid at the Medical City was a great loss to the hospitals and especially to our humanitarian work in Iraq.

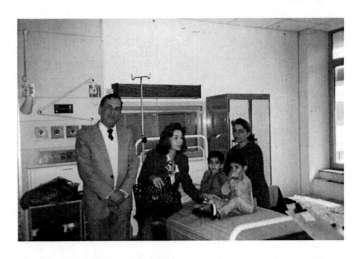

Dr Khalid Al Obaydi, member of MAIC's medical team in Iraq, and May Al-Daftari visiting a children's ward at Central Paediatric Teaching Hospital, Medical City, Baghdad, February 1996.

May Al-Daftari meeting with members of MAIC medical team in Iraq. From left: Dr Hussam Charmougli, Dr Ihsan Al Bahrani and Dr Khalid Al Obaydi on May's left. Al Mansour Paediatric Teaching Hospital, Baghdad, February 1996.

Dr Ihsan Al Bahrani MD, Professor and Leading Cardiologist in Iraq, Director of Cardiology Departments in Several Teaching Hospitals, President of the Board of Governors for Heart Diseases at the Ministry of Higher Education Between 2005 and 2008

The late Dr Al Bahrani was married to my sister Sevim and I am lucky that I had him as my brother-in-law. He had a long history with the Medical City in Baghdad and with its hospitals and University. He was highly respected, especially amongst doctors, most of whom had been his students.

Ihsan helped MAIC from the start of our operation in recommending the members for MAIC's Medical Team in Iraq. He also joined the team in 1997 and stayed until 2008, when he moved to Amman and became an honorary member of MAIC.

I will never forget his extensive assistance to the charity. He not only offered valuable advice, helped me tour the hospitals and facilitated my meetings with doctors, he was also our first line of contact in Iraq. He would be the first to inform us of the arrival of the charity's medical supplies and the progress of their distribution to the assigned hospitals.

Sadly, I lost my dear brother-in-law following an illness in 2016.

Mr Hussein Malik, MD Paediatric Surgeon at the Central Paediatric Teaching Hospital (Al Tifal Al Markazi, Baghdad)

During my visit to Baghdad in 1995, Khalid introduced me to Hussein Malik, a young paediatric surgeon working at the Central Paediatric Teaching Hospital. Hussein is a graduate of the Medical University in Iraq and spoke very good English. During my visit to the hospital, he accompanied me around the wards and was very thorough in explaining the medical condition of each child. Hussein had a kind and warm personality. He showed a special fondness for children and had a caring approach as he spoke to the sick children.

On my return to London, I stayed in contact with him and was impressed by his feedback regarding our aid to the hospital. MAIC Board members were very pleased with his cooperation and we invited him in 1998 to join the charity's Medical Team in Iraq. His significant contribution to the charity continued until 2006 when he and his family left for Syria during the period when many doctors were targeted by terrorists and kidnappers and killed or kidnapped for high ransoms. After a few months, he returned to Baghdad and to his work at the Central Paediatric Teaching Hospital.

We invited Hussein to London to be one of the speakers at MAIC's forum "Health of Children in Iraq" on 3 May 2005 at the Royal Geographical Society. We also offered him a two-month training programme at the Chelsea and Westminster Hospital in London, where he specialised in child laparoscopy. He continued his affiliation with MAIC until the closure of the charity in 2009. Sadly, Dr Hussein Malik passed away in 2016 after a short illness.

Dr Jawad Khadem Al Ali MD, Expert Oncologist at Basrah Hospital, Basrah, Currently a Member of the Iraqi Cancer Board and Working at Alsadr Teaching Hospital

Jawad joined MAIC's Medical Team in 1998 and was a very valuable member of the charity. He provided information on the rise of cancers and the hospital's need for cancer treatments. His research on cancer is very significant in evaluating its causes and treatment. MAIC offered to publish his research and unfortunately, after initial agreement, Jawad decided not to go through with it.

Jawad gave a very powerful and disturbing presentation at MAIC's forum on the "Health of Children in Iraq" on 3 May 2005. He discussed the effects of post-war environmental contamination on health in Iraq. He showed pictures of children suffering from different types of cancers, some with multiple cancers as well as deformities.

In his recent communication below, Jawad reviews the present conditions of cancer patients and their dilemmas in receiving treatment.

Dear Mrs. May Aldaftari

Thank you for your greetings. Me and my family are well. I wish you the best of times and good health.

I am still working in the hospital as an expert oncologist and am still a member of the Iraqi Cancer Board. My work is mainly based at Alsadr Teaching Hospital. My work mainly focuses on treating advanced cases of cancer in adults and dealing with the complications that come up during treatment. We register about 2,500 cases annually in our center. About 50–55 patients die monthly because of lack of medicines, which are not supplied by the Ministry of Health. Some patients buy their medicine on their own, but usually its cost is very high and poor patients can't afford the price of costly drugs. Laboratories won't provide most of the tests required for patients. Instruments are available but materials for tests and maintenance are not available.

The staff are not well trained and their number has been reduced to a minimum because of our small budget.

My best regards
Yours Dr Jawad Al Ali

Dr Mazin Al Jadiry, Consultant Oncologist at the Children's Welfare Teaching Hospital (Previously Known as Al Mansour Paediatric Teaching Hospital), Medical City, Baghdad

When I first met Mazin, it was in 1997 at the Al Mansour Paediatric Teaching Hospital, where he was a young Oncologist in the cancer ward. His attentive and perceptive manner and his well-organised collection of patients' records were very impressive.

We kept in touch and saw him on my later visits. His input to the charity was very useful, especially after the departure of Khalid Al Obaydi from the hospital in 2004.

He was appointed as a member of the MAIC Medical Team in 2007. In the same year, we offered him a short training programme at Alder Hay Hospital in Liverpool.

I am still in contact with him. In our last communication, after I had inquired about present conditions in the hospital, he stated that although conditions are better in general, there are discrepancies in supplies. He continued to say, 'Medications are expensive, and at the same time, the most usable and cheap medications are not available.'

Dr Ihsan Al Bahrani, a member of MAIC's medical team in Iraq, and May Al-Daftari inspecting a Drager incubator donated by MAIC to the hospital in 1998. Central Paediatric Teaching Hospital, Baghdad, October 1998.

Dr Hussain Malik, member of MAIC's medical team in Iraq, and May Al-Daftari meeting with medical staff at the hospital. Central Paediatric Teaching Hospital, Baghdad, September 2000.

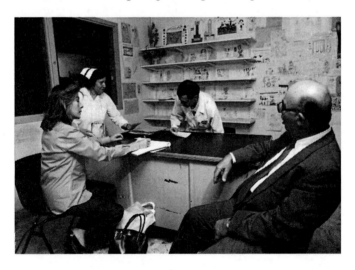

May A Daftari and Dr Ihsan Al Bahrani visiting Dr Mazin Al Jadiry, oncologist at the Cancer Unit at Al Mansour Teaching Hospital. Baghdad, September 2000.

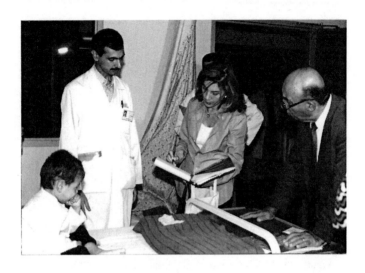

Reviewing the condition of a young cancer patient in remission. From left: Dr Mazin Al Jadiry, the hospital's oncologist, May Al-Daftari and Dr Ihsan Al Bahrani. Al Mansour Paediatric Teaching Hospital, Baghdad, September 2000.

Dr Jawad Al Ali, oncologist at Basrah Teaching Hospital and a member of MAIC medical team in Iraq, visiting the charity's office in London and meeting with Fatima Sheikh Khazaal, Trustee, and May Al-Daftari. London, 3 May 2005.

Chapter 6
Effects of 2003 Gulf War
on Iraqis and MAIC

The second Gulf War which started on 19 March 2003 and lasted three weeks, brought about the overthrow of the Baath rule and occupation by the coalition forces, principally the United States and Great Britain, until a national government could be formed. The Coalition Provisional Authority (CPA)was established until sovereignty was transferred to an Interim Iraqi Government in June 2004.

During the period between 2003 and the closure of MAIC in 2009, new conditions and regulations for charitable work prevailed in the country which required urgent attention of aid organisations to reconsider their work procedures in order to cope with the new changes. Needless to say, MAIC had to do likewise. The most serious problems we faced immediately after the 2003 Gulf War were the following:

- The first serious problem that MAIC confronted while Iraq was under occupation was the loss of significant quantities of medical supplies. The supplies had been taken to Iraq by Virgin Atlantic Airlines, together with supplies from other donors, as part of the first British humanitarian flight on 1 May 2003, after the Second Gulf War. The flight landed in Basrah and our supplies were handed over to the British forces to be distributed to our assigned hospitals in Iraq. Unfortunately, as we found later, a large number of medical items went missing.

- Charities had to go through a new set of regulations and deal with different bodies. At the beginning, MAIC had had to work through the occupation representatives, the Iraq Medical Assistance Committee (IMAC), but after June 2004, this changed to the Iraqi Ministry of Health (MOH).

- Health wise the brutal war increased further the misery and misfortune of an already drained and vulnerable population. It raised environmental pollution levels, contaminating drinking water. Serious injuries also multiplied, due to the number of scattered bomblets and unexploded ordnance everywhere. Children and young adults, who used open spaces more than older adults, were most likely to be affected by these injuries, which often resulted in lifelong disability. This group also suffered most intensely from the agonising trauma of living in war zones. The post-war situation necessitated that MAIC increase and diversify its regular medicines and provide extra treatments for children with injuries both physical and psychological.

- Following the regime change, many doctors were replaced due to their political affiliations. Thousands left the country due to the chaos and the rise of militias which targeted and kidnapped doctors and medical staff. Three members of MAIC's Medical Team in Iraq were affected by these conditions.

I will discuss the above points in more detail in the following pages.

Lost Supplies

A relatively large consignment of medical supplies of over £200,000 in value was planned prior to the second Gulf War, in anticipation of hospitals' likely needs in the event of war breaking out. The delay in approvals and the time-consuming process of compiling the supplies prevented us from sending the consignment on time.

In April 2003, the supplies were ready, packed and labelled with the names of the five receiving hospitals: Al Mansour Paediatric Teaching Hospital, Kadisya General Hospital, Paediatric Section, Kerbala Children's Hospital, the Central Paediatric Teaching Hospital and Basrah Teaching Hospital. The consignment was at the warehouse of Durbin PLC, which is the charity's main medical supplier.

At the end of April, we were contacted by Lilian Darko from Durbin and informed that Virgin Atlantic Airways was preparing the first emergency humanitarian aid after the war, which was to be airlifted to Iraq. We were also told that some of the medical items on the coalition's list of urgent needs were included in our consignment. For this reason, Virgin would give MAIC priority to transport its supplies free of charge to Basrah. Our response was that we would consider the offer once we received confirmation from the official occupying forces that they would take responsibility for handling the consignment and distributing it to the assigned five hospitals.

Watermark, Virgin's publicity company, was responsible for coordinating with different aid suppliers to compile a humanitarian aid cargo to be delivered to the coalition forces in Basrah. Through Durbin we received on 29 April 2003 a written confirmation from John Caulcutt at Watermark stating that the consignment would be delivered to the nominated hospitals. He wrote: 'I would like to tell you that we have been assured, by the Coalition Forces, that this will be the case.' (See Appendix 16.) We also demanded a confirmation letter from the receiving coalition officer in charge. The British Colonel John Graham, Commander Medical, Middle East, who was stationed in Basrah, wrote on 2 May 2003 and confirmed the receipt of the consignment, its safe storage and distribution. 'We are able to arrange immediate safe storage of the medicines and equipment and they will be moved very shortly to the intended recipients.' (See Appendix 17.)

A few weeks passed and there was no news of the delivery to the hospitals. I wrote to John Graham several times between 19 May and 10 July and pressed him to accelerate the distribution as most of the medicines were heat-sensitive and were urgently needed by the hospitals. Although Basrah Hospital was the first to receive supplies after a couple of weeks, unfortunately it only received 44 per cent of the value of its assigned items. Delivery to the remaining hospitals was delayed for a few more weeks and regrettably on delivery, their boxes were already unwrapped and a large proportion of the items were missing. Most of the wheelchairs and crutches had not been delivered. After investigating the matter further and asking our doctors in the hospitals to fill in a checklist, we found that the value of the missing supplies exceeded £98,000.

The loss of approximately half of MAIC's consignment was most distressing for the members of the charity. Not only did it deprive children of lifesaving treatments and anti-cancer drugs, but it meant that funds were lost which had been raised nationwide by people who had sacrificed and worked hard to sponsor the consignment. Hence it was vital to seek compensation from the British government as the consignment had been handled by the British health officer Colonel John Graham.

On 20 October 2003, I wrote to the Prime Minister, Tony Blair, explaining the problem. My letter was acknowledged on 23 October and forwarded to a minister at the Department of International Development (DIFD), asking him to reply to me directly. Sadly, the reply I received from Hilary Benn, a minister at DIFD, was not satisfactory.

On 15 December 2003, I received a letter from RT Hon. Adam Ingram MP at the Ministry of Armed Forces MoD in response to my letter to Hilary Benn. (See Appendix 18.) After acknowledging John Graham's letter, he wrote: 'The UK Divisional HQ received the medicines and equipment on 2 May, stored them safely and undertook to arrange their passage to the intendent recipients. However, we have no record of any understanding to deliver equipment or medicines to hospitals across Iraq or obtain receipts for their delivery.' He continued in another paragraph, 'In this case the supplies arrived with British Forces in Basra unsolicited.

Rather than have them returned to the UK, Colonel Graham made his best endeavours in the difficult circumstances pertaining at the time to have them delivered to the intended recipients in good faith.' He also stated, 'Where the hospitals were located in other parts of the country, Korean Food for the Hungry took possession of the supplies for onward dispatch.'

In my reply to Adam Ingram of 22 December 2003 (see Appendix 19), I challenged the points raised by him and also repeated my understanding of John Graham's assurances of undertaking the safe distribution of the consignment in his capacity as Commander Medical of the British Forces in Basra. I also questioned the delivery procedure of the supplies to the Basrah Hospital which was in the same city where he was stationed. The hospital received only £29,367.50 worth of supplies out of a total value of £65,496.99. I wrote: 'As Basrah has been under British control, I did not think it was unreasonable to expect Colonel Graham to arrange safe delivery of our supplies to the Basrah Hospital and to acquire a delivery receipt.' I also listed a breakdown of the value of the missing items for the remaining four hospitals, which totalled £98,784.49, the amount for which MAIC was seeking compensation.

We continued the communications in January and February 2004, but Adam Ingram repeatedly denied any responsibility of the MoD in the loss of the charity's supplies. Sadly, MAIC was unable to receive any compensation from the MoD.

The story of the charity's lost supplies was covered in the media. Sky News aired the story on 27 October 2003 after visiting the charity's office in London. The programme was presented by Peter Sharp. The *Independent* published an article by Robert Fisk on 30 December 2003: 'UK Charity Seeks Compensation Over Lost Cancer drugs for Iraqi Children.'

What was most touching was the humane and honourable response of many members of the British public, who not only sent donations, but also sympathetic letters expressing their dismay about what had happened and their willingness to raise funds to compensate MAIC's loss.

New Regulations for Charity Donations

Following the war and during 2003, new regulations for receiving charitable donations were introduced. All prospective donations had to go through the Iraqi Medical Assistance Committee (IMAC), which included representatives from the Coalition Provisional Authority (CPA), the Iraqi Ministry of Health (MOH), the UN (WHO, UNICEF and UNFPA), the NGO community, the International Red Cross/Red Crescent (ICRC) and the donor community (DFID and USAID). (See Appendix 20.) This meant that we had to deal with another set of bureaucratic regulations in order to carry on sending medical supplies to hospitals in Iraq.

As of March 2004, IMAC handed over its responsibilities to the International Affairs Department in the Ministry of Health (see Appendix 21). Once again, MAIC had to adjust to the latest change of regulations, some of which created distribution problems for the charity. Nevertheless, we were able to deliver twenty-two consignments of medical supplies to paediatric hospitals between 2004 and 2009. The lifting of sanctions did help to speed up the approvals and send a larger variety of medical supplies to Iraq, yet the new regulations created problems of distribution to hospitals. The Iraqi MOH regulations required that charity donations should be handed over to a MOH agency for distribution. The by-laws of MAIC dictated that aid supplies should be delivered to hospitals and not to government agencies. This conflict resulted in us delivering supplies to fewer hospitals, whose directors belonged to either an affluent political party or a religious group. They facilitated the entry of their consignment through customs and took delivery of the supplies themselves. Other less fortunate hospitals with no connections, such as a hospital in Mosul which had benefited from MAIC's aid in the past, refused to receive aid from the charity for fear of raising problems with the MOH, even though this hospital was in desperate need of medical supplies.

Effects of the 2003 Gulf War on Iraqis

A population worn out by poverty, malnutrition and disease during thirteen years of harsh sanctions was subjected once more to a war that had worse tragic consequences.

The 2003 Gulf War increased the damage to an already rundown utilities network, especially water and electricity systems. Sanitation problems became a major source for the spread of infectious diseases. Certain areas became contaminated by human waste. Many schools and hospitals did not have access to clean potable water. The polluted water led to the rise of waterborne diseases such as malaria, typhoid fever, hepatitis and cholera among the population, children as always being the most vulnerable.

The pollution to the environment caused by the use of lethal weapons during the war resulted in the appearance of a new and strange phenomena of cancers in the form of cluster cancers in families and double and triple cancers in individuals. Dr Jawad Al Ali in his address at MAIC's Forum on 3 May 2005, attributed these changes in cancers to the excessive use of depleted uranium in the past two wars.

Another painful consequence of the war and its aftermath was the dramatic rise in disabilities caused by injuries. Scores of people lost limbs and many others their vision. Thousands of people were killed and maimed not only during the airstrike but also as a result of the confrontation and exchange of fire between the multinational forces and the Iraqis. The multinational forces in search of insurgents, broke into the homes of Iraqis and fired on their inhabitants. Many of the victims were women and children. (More information on the situation can be read in the article by Dr Burhan Gilbert from John Hopkins Bloomberg School of Public Health, which was published in the *Lancet Medical Journal*, Edition 14, October 2006.)

Other major sources of injuries to children were uncleared explosive remnants of the war and the cluster bomblets, which spread out across the open fields where thousands of children played and got injured.

The trauma of living in a war zone and the conflict situation which followed between multinational forces and Iraqis and militias which belonged to different Iraqi political or religious groups had enormous psychological effects on children. They witnessed these bloody encounters as well as the forced evacuations of their families, abductions of family members, and sometimes even the death or injury of one or both parents or siblings. Moreover, deadly explosions and suicide bombings by different sectarian factions were taking place daily all over Iraq, killing and maiming scores of innocent adults and children.

Millions of children were traumatised and the majority of them suffered from a psychological condition known as Post Traumatic Stress Disorder (PTSD). Unfortunately, child psychiatrists were very rare in Iraq at that time, let alone specialists in this field. Prior to the war, UNICEF estimated that over 500,000 children would require psychiatric help in case of war. Given that over a million children were orphaned, it seems likely that the UNICEF figure was an underestimate and didn't include these children, many of whom needed psychological help as well as urgently requiring shelter, care, love and a decent life. They suffered in silence and lived under heart breaking conditions, with very little help being offered.

Once the war was over and contact was resumed with MAIC's doctors, we were overwhelmed by the colossal and urgent requirements of the hospitals which were treating sick and injured children. We increased the quantities of our regular medicines such as anti-cancer drugs, third-generation antibiotics, surgical items, blood bags, transfusion sets and saline solutions. We also included anaesthetics, prosthetics supplies, raw material for splints, suspension belts and vacuum-forming machines, wheelchairs and crutches. Due to the looting of hospitals that followed the war, much equipment such as diagnostic machines and instruments as well as laboratory equipment was urgently needed. We tried to replace what we could with the limited funds we had, managing to restore to the hospitals items including: Radiometer, its reagents and electrodes; a Fluoroscopy machine; a Mini Vidas automated immune-analyser; paediatric laparoscopic instruments; and different spare parts for equipment which had been donated earlier by MAIC.

The psychiatric help required for Iraqi children was the most worrying and difficult need the charity tried to address. With the absence of professional personnel in this field in Iraq, it was beyond our capacity as a small charity to make a tangible difference. However, with the help of the late Dr Jack Piachaud, a well-known consultant psychiatrist in London, we were able in 2005 to offer short training programmes for five Iraqi doctors, among them three psychiatrists. We were most grateful to Jack for his valuable assistance in raising funds for the travelling and accommodation costs of the doctors and for their placements in specialized hospitals: the NHS and Social Care Trust in West Kent, the Northampton Hospital, the Maudsley Hospital, the Great Ormond Street Hospital and the Chelsea and Westminster Hospital, the last three in London. In 2006 and 2007, with the sponsorship from the Karim Rida Said Foundation (KRSF), to whom we are also most grateful, we were able to offer one-month training programmes to four paediatric doctors, one at the Hammersmith Hospital in London, two at Adler Hay Hospital in Liverpool and one at St Mary Department of Paediatric Haematology in London. Although most of the training offered by the hospitals was given as observative training, the Iraqi doctors benefited a great deal.

Changes That Affected MAIC's Medical Team in Iraq

The new government that was formed after the war and the toppling of President Saddam Hussein and the Baath regime replaced all high-ranking officials working at ministries, government institutions and also at hospitals. Dr Khalid Al Obaydi, a valued member of the charity's Medical Team, was relieved from his post as Director of the Medical City and appointed to an alternative post until he left Iraq for

Abu Dhabi in 2006. As a result, we lost one of our most efficient doctors at the Welfare Paediatric Teaching Hospital.

The breakdown of security that followed the war gave rise to a dangerous situation of abductions and kidnappings by different groups of militias demanding ransom money. Doctors and medical staff were the main target. My brother in-law, the late Dr Ihssan Al Bahrani, the most valued member of MAIC's Medical Team, was kidnapped in 2005 and remained in captivity for over a week, while his abductors were negotiating ransom money with my sister. It was an ugly nightmare and a scary experience for Ihssan, my sister and the rest of the family. Thank God he was released and after his ordeal left Iraq with my sister and settled in Amman.

In 2006, when doctors were still targeted, Dr Hussein Malik, another valued member of the Medical Team, left Iraq with his young family and stayed in Syria for a few months as he feared that either he or his young boys might be abducted. We were fortunate that he returned to his work at the Central Paediatric Teaching hospital and resumed his valuable presence on the charity's Medical Team in Iraq.

Following these changes, MAIC appointed Dr Mazin Al Jadiry to the Medical Team. I had met Dr Al Jadiry during my previous trips and visits to the Welfare Paediatric Teaching Hospital. His assistance and commitment to the values and objectives of the charity were highly appreciated.

The worrying security issues and the continued explosions and suicide bombings in different parts of Iraq remained to be major concerns until the winding-up of MAIC in 2009.

On a positive note, the lifting of sanctions in May 2003 had facilitated MAIC's humanitarian aid to hospitals. It sped up the approvals process required to send medical aid to Iraqi hospitals. It also improved the means of shipment and made it easier, as the ban on flights to and from Iraq was removed, allowing the charity to ship its consignments directly to Iraq by air. We were also able to offer short training programmes between 2005 and 2007 to nine Iraqi doctors at UK hospitals.

After more than a decade of deprivation in medical advances, the training programmes in the UK offered Iraqi doctors, opportunities to observe the latest techniques used in the treatments administered in child malignancy diseases and stress disorders, two of the main diseases suffered by Iraqi children. Some doctors also attended training in paediatric laparoscopic surgery.

The doctors were well pleased with their training and returned home with stacks of medical books and journals. They shared their acquired knowledge with their colleagues at the Iraqi hospitals.

Chapter 7
Funding, Donors and Fundraising Events

MAIC's funds grew from my small initial donation of £10,000, made in 1995, to £3.7 million collected over fourteen years, up until the closure of the charity in 2009. It is a modest amount, especially when compared to many other charities, where this figure could be collected in one year, or sometimes even in one fundraising event.

However, what made MAIC different from other charities was that a large proportion of the source of funds came from small donations made by people with limited resources. They worked tirelessly and put great effort into raising funds from activities to help our charity. Some donors even deprived themselves of comforts they could have used the money for, preferring to donate it instead to MAIC.

During the first three months, we raised £90,000 in donations which came mainly from friends and acquaintances, a few charitable organisations and the charity's fundraising events. By the end of the year, the funds had reached £154,000.

In the later years, the funds raised each year increased due to the expansion of our donor base and the increase in MAIC's fundraising activities, especially its annual dinners.

MAIC's long list of supporters included British and Arab donors, who regularly attended the charity's fundraising events and sponsored significant parts of its medical consignments. It also included donations from humanitarian agencies, foundations, corporates, churches, schools and universities. A large portion of funding also came from individuals who undertook activities in support of the charity such as art exhibitions, concerts, sponsored runs, and making and selling goods. Many others sent donations on family occasions, when celebrating weddings, the births of babies, birthdays and retirements. These generous people gave up their presents and advised family and friends to donate instead to MAIC and help children who were less fortunate and in need. Many donors sent their donations through our account with Charities Aid Foundation (CAF) which is a registered UK charity that lists UK charities on its website.

Funding and Donors

Unlike many charities, MAIC had no reserve funds. It had to raise funds in advance of each medical consignment, especially during an emergency period where hospitals were in dire conditions and the need to send medical supplies to save children was of utmost urgency. Donors and fundraisers were the lifeline of the charity. Without them we could not have funded our medical consignments and saved thousands of young lives.

From the Charity's large spectrum of donors, I have chosen as examples three aid organisations which played a significant role in funding and a few selfless individuals, who had special and touching stories of sacrifice. I will also highlight MAIC's main fundraising activities.

The Department for International Development (DFID)

In 1996, we were contacted by The Overseas Development Administration (ODA) in London (whose name changed later to the Department for International Development (DFID)) and invited to a meeting with ODA personnel. I went with Soad and Sabah to the meeting, where we were briefed about the work of the ODA and were told about the availability of funds to support humanitarian projects in Iraq. A few days later, we presented the ODA with a short list of medical supplies which were urgently needed by the hospitals. The consignment was valued at £54,600. We were very happy to find that the ODA approved our list and we received £22,500, which was the ODA's first grant to MAIC. They continued to make donations to help fund our medical supplies for a further three years as DFID. Their donations to MAIC increased to £40,000 in 1997, £45,000 in 1998 and £190,000 in 1999. DFID remained one of our major sponsors during the time of the Conservative government.

Unfortunately, the Department changed its policy of supporting MAIC once Labour won the General Election and the Labour government took over. Previously in 1998, during the term of the Conservative government, we had an agreement with DIFID to sponsor a large part of our medical consignment, valued then at £225,000, which was earmarked for seven paediatric hospitals in Iraq. Soon after the Labour government was formed, new personnel replaced the old at DFID. In 1999, when payment was due to the supplier, we contacted DFID to pay their agreed share of funding. To our surprise, we were told that our files could not be found and nor could any communication from our charity. We were desperate to get the funding in order to settle the invoice of the supplier. We photocopied the whole file of our correspondence with the DFID over three years and sent it, together with the relevant documents showing DFID's approval for sponsoring large parts of the consignment, to their offices. Although in the end, DFID did pay the agreed funds, unfortunately it was their last donation.

The Karim Rida Said Foundation (KRSF)

KRSF was another major supporter whose yearly funding was uninterrupted from 1995 until 2008, totalling over £250,000. As well as their yearly donation towards medical supplies, the KRSF sponsored some of our charity's training projects between 2005 and 2009, which offered Iraqi doctors the opportunity to attend short training programmes at UK hospitals.

The Foundation also organised a yearly drawing competition for children from different countries and invited sick children at Iraqi hospitals to send their drawings and enter the competition. Dr Khalid and Dr Hussein, both members of

MAIC, used to send the children's drawings to London, which was a complicated and time-consuming task. They had to find someone who was travelling by land to carry the drawings, as flights in and out of Iraq were prohibited. However, it was well worth the trouble as it brought much happiness to our young cancer patients and encouraged them to be creative and look forward to joining an exciting and competitive event. Although the Iraqi children did not have the variety of coloured pencils or the fine drawing paper that children in some of the other countries had, their drawings were beautiful and expressive, with an underlying tone of sadness; they reflected their poor and unhappy surroundings. Many of them won the first and second prizes. What a joy it was when we bought them clothes, games and little gadgets with their prize money and imagined the excitement they would feel upon receiving their gifts.

The Ousseimi Foundation

The Ousseimi Foundation was another committed supporter that commenced its donations in 2000 and continued with them until 2008. The Foundation's contributions were substantial, totalling over £250,000 and including sponsored medicines and much-needed equipment.

Individuals, Schools and Groups with Special Stories

From the long list of MAIC's donors I have chosen the following dedicated and passionate people for their special stories:

Reverend John Stephenson from the Church of St Chad in Sunderland (ex-vicar of All Saints' Church, Eppleton)

Reverend John Stephenson started raising funds for MAIC in June 2001 and continued until the closure of the charity. His weekly contributions amounted to over £16,000 over a period of eight years. They were raised from writing and selling booklets for £1.50 and from the collections he made from hundreds of donors in the church congregation and supporters. He wrote poetry and prose expressing his pain and anger for the calamities of the war that had befallen the Iraqis and in particular the children. He remained committed to helping the sick children until the closure of the charity in 2009. (See Appendix 22.)

The St Chad Church, and especially its vicar, Jeremy Chadd, who with Mrs Chadd sent generous donations, were also very supportive of MAIC.

In 2004 I received an invitation from St Chad Church to give the Sunday sermon on 2 May that year and talk to the congregation about our charity's humanitarian aid in Iraq. I was deeply touched by this kind gesture of compassion, which allowed me, as a Muslim, to give this sacred service usually given by a priest. Fatima Khazaal, a trustee of MAIC, and myself arrived in East Herrington in Sunderland and were met by Reverend Stephenson. It was the first time we had met face to face after three years of receiving his passionate letters with which he also sent poetry books and generous donations. He was surprised to see us unveiled and said he was looking for two ladies with black head covers. He later took us around to see his village and served us tea at the home of Mrs Joan Newport, a wonderful lady from the parish. She was very generous and so kind that she gave us her only bedroom to sleep in that night. The second morning, we all headed to the Church. Before reviewing the humanitarian work of the charity, I started my address by expressing my gratitude and appreciation to the congregation and attendants. They were mainly a mining community who had suffered great financial difficulties due to the closure of their mines a few decades previously, yet they were very passionate and generous in their offering to MAIC. Then I spoke about the ancient Christian communities which had settled in Iraq as early as the second century and their valued contribution to the intellectual and historical environment of Iraq.

After the sermon, communion and blessings were offered by the clergy. The parish of St Chad's joined together in prayers to ease the pain of the children in Iraq. The attendants showed great concern for the misfortune of Iraqis and the suffering of the children.

Dr Mercy Heatley

Dr Mercy Heatley was a paediatric psychiatrist with a special interest in children with autism. She lived in Oxford and had a long history of campaigning for peace, helping refugees and people displaced by war in Europe. Her contribution to MAIC was not only financial, but also an expression of human values. In 2002, at the age of eighty, she made national news when she withheld 7 per cent of her personal income tax in protest at the war on Iraq. She donated an equal amount to MAIC to buy penicillin to treat children in Iraqi hospitals. Her reasoning was that she wanted to disassociate herself from the war and she explained her behaviour by saying that she refused to fund the bombs that killed Iraqis and chose instead to send Penicillin to save Iraqi children.

She invited me to her home in Old Marston, Oxford, to meet her husband, Dr Norman Heatley. I was privileged to meet this great person who was 91 years old and the last survivor of the famous Oxford Team, under the directorship of Professor Howard Florey, which had worked hard to produce penicillin during the Second World War as many injured Allied soldiers were dying from infected wounds. They cultivated the penicillin in bed pans and used it for trial on the first patient in 1941. With this great breakthrough, penicillin was produced in commercial quantities in the USA. It was used for the first time in large quantities in 1942, and it treated and saved thousands of injured soldiers. With this background Dr Mercy wanted to send Penicillin to save young Iraqi lives.

During the meeting, I showed them the DTI application form and explained the process involved in obtaining UN approval to send medicines to Iraq. Dr Mercy presented me with her donation cheque to sponsor antibiotics for children's hospitals in Iraq. The meeting was filmed on Central News, one of Oxford's TV channels. An interesting article on the Heatleys was published in the *Oxford Mail* on 2 February 2002. (See Appendix 23.)

A souvenir photo with members of St Chad Church. From left: Mrs Joan Newport, Reverend John Stephenson, May Al-Daftari and Vicar Jeremy Chad. Sunderland, May 2004.

Meeting with Drs Mercy and Norman Heatley and going through the UN application forms to seek approval to donate penicillin, the antibiotic they wanted to send to Iraq. Oxford, February 2002.

Dr Mercy remained active and regularly sent donations and medical journals (such as the *BMJ*) to Iraqi doctors through MAIC. Sending the journals was a lengthy process. We had to list every single issue in our application to the DTI to get the necessary approval to be able to send them. She also helped many Iraqi doctors stranded in the UK following the 2003 war who were in financial difficulties, and others looking for jobs or training in UK hospitals. Her weak health did not stop her from supporting MAIC until 2009 by networking even when she was bedridden. Dr Mercy Heatley passed away on 5 September 2016 at the age of ninety-four, leaving behind a legacy of exceptional human values.

Nicola Greenwood and Martin Wyatt

A self-denying couple who were deeply moved by the suffering of Iraqi children. Their story is one of compassion and selflessness in support of MAIC.

Nicola was originally a dancer and became a soloist soprano. She sang with St Gregory's Choral Society and UEA-based Peter Aston Singers and later on, she formed the Greenwood Singers.

Martin Wyatt was a musical director, conductor and the founder of the St Gregory's Orchestra, which was formed in 1986.

In 2003 Nicola contacted MAIC to gain approval for a fundraising benefit concert for MAIC. This was the first of several concerts given later by St Gregory's Orchestra in which both Nicola and Martin performed to help the children in Iraq.

On 18 September 2005, Nicola and Martin were married at the United Reform Church in Norwich. Their wedding invitation read, 'No presents just your presence. Donations to Medical Aid for Iraqi Children: We have everything, they have nothing.' (See Appendix 24.) What can one add to this show of sacrifice and to their deep sense of devotion towards Iraqi children?

Over the years they continued with their concerts to support MAIC until I learned from Martin in 2009 the heartbreaking news that Nicola, unfortunately, was very sick, suffering from Multiple Sclerosis (MS). Although Martin was devastated, yet he wrote to express his sadness for the winding-up of MAIC and also praised the charity's achievements in saving children's lives over the past years. It was painful and heart-touching to read his letter and realise how caring Martin and Nicola were and how much MAIC meant to them at a time when they themselves needed sympathy and support.

The Students of the City of London School for Girls

The students of the City of London School for Girls raised substantial funds through their Appeal Fund for MAIC, which ran throughout the academic year 2006–2007.

East House at Bancroft's School

The pupils of East House at Bancroft's School, Woodford Green in Essex chose MAIC as one of their two nominated charities for the academic year 2007–2008 and raised a significant amount of funds during two fundraising events organised by the students.

Exotix Ltd/ICAP Plc

In 2006 the employees of Exotix Ltd chose MAIC as a beneficiary for their annual charity day, where the employees gave the fees they earned in a whole day to charity.

Lee Mulvihill

He donated his fees from an interview published in the *Daily Mirror* in memory of his late wife, Flight Lieutenant Sarah-Jayne Mulvihill, who lost her life in a helicopter crash in Iraq.

Sofia Tierney

Sofia, a little girl of six, was so upset when she watched television during the 2003 war and saw little Iraqi children suffering in hospital beds. She told her mother that she did not want presents on her seventh birthday and would prefer to send toys to Iraqi children instead. MAIC received several donations from her family and friends. A few more young girls followed suit as many young children or their parents read these stories in our newsletters and on our website.

Lanai Collis

Lanai was the youngest donor; she donated her sixth birthday gifts to MAIC.

Country Runs

Students and young adults participated in runs in different counties to raise funds for MAIC. The runs included the Annual BUPA Great North Run, the Great Escape Run (Imperial College) and the Great Manchester Run.

These stories and many others of devotion and sacrifices to ease the suffering of Iraqi children are most humbling. It also encourages us to believe in the existence of a strong human bond between people wherever they are, unrestricted by their race or religion.

These donors and many more like them, no matter how small or large their donations were, did save many young lives and provided treatment to thousands of sick children. As I am writing those lines, I am reflecting on how a cannula worth about thirty pence or a course of antibiotics priced at £6 saved the life of a sick child during the crippling sanctions when medicines and surgical items were nearly non-existent. These donors deserve all our respect and gratitude.

These stories remind me of the precious words of Mother Teresa: 'Not all of us can do great things. But we can do small things with great love.'

Members of MAIC Board of Governors at "Art and Draw" fund-raising event. Conducting the draw from left to right: Salma Sambar, Doris Riachy and Randa Smadi. London, 21 November 1996.

MAIC's members at the Charity's Annual Dinner at the Dorchester Hotel. London, 18 June 1997.

MAIC members representing the charity at "Day for the People of Iraq" held at Kensington Town Hall. London, 6 May 2000.

MAIC members Maysa Ibrahim and Tamima Ismail conducting a draw at "Iftar Meal" at Noura Restaurant. London, 16 November 2002.

MAIC members at work during "Iftar Meal" at Noura Restaurant. From left to right: Dunia Farman Farmaian, May Achour, Doris Riachy, Fatima Sheikh Khazaal, May Al-Daftari, Bassam Zaku, (Emma, Secretary) and Joan Khan. London, 16 November 2002.

MAIC's Fundraising Events

In addition to the generous channels of donations outlined earlier, MAIC's fundraising activities were also an important source of funding.

Starting with the charity's inauguration evening on 6 May 1995 at the Mayfair InterContinental Hotel, London, which was attended by 350 guests and raised generous donations, MAIC continued with fundraising events. Its activities included annual dinners, as well as small events, such as Art and Draw, bazaars and Iftars (evening meals where people broke their fasts during the month of Ramadan). We also had ladies' lunches that took place at the homes of generous ladies who opened their homes and sponsored the meals.

All these events, whether small or large, were well attended by generous supporters who helped to sponsor the charity's much needed humanitarian consignments.

MAIC's Annual Dinners

Following the inauguration event in 1995, MAIC was privileged to have the support of highly esteemed and renowned guest speakers to address the attendants at the charity's annual dinners.

On 16 January 1996, MAIC was honoured to have Mr Nazar Kabbani, the renowned Arab poet, to give a poetry recital at the Royal Geographical Society. The late Mr Kabbani was very ill and only rarely accepted poetry invitations during his last years of illness. He was deeply moved by the agony of the Iraqi people and made a great effort to attend and support our cause. He gave a most powerful poetry recital, which was sadly his last public appearance before he passed away.

On 18 June 1997, MAIC held its annual dinner at the Dorchester Hotel, London.

Layla Pachachi, a mezzo soprano, donated a wonderful recital of Carmen, the opera by Georges Bizet. We were most appreciative of Layla's kind generosity.

On 27 May 1998, MAIC held its Annual Dinner at the Dorchester Hotel, London. We were very fortunate to have the support of the late Mr Robert Fisk, as the guest speaker. The respected master of truthful journalism, Mr Fisk spoke of the painful suffering of Iraqi children and painted a bleak picture of the long-term effects of the war on them.

On 27 May 1999, MAIC's annual dinner again took place at the Dorchester Hotel. We were grateful to have Mr George Galloway (MP for Glasgow, Kevin at the time) as the guest speaker. He gave a very moving speech and highlighted the rise in cancers and deformities in children after the first Gulf War.

On 1 April 2000, MAIC celebrated its fifth anniversary with entertainment held at the Dorchester Hotel, London. Keynote speeches were given by the charity's members and substantial sums were raised on the evening.

On 9 May 2001, under the royal patronage of Her Majesty Queen Rania Al-Abdullah of Jordan, we held MAIC's annual dinner at the Brewery, London. It was a great honour to have

Her Majesty's support of our humanitarian cause. In her speech, Her Majesty emphasised the suffering of Iraqi children under sanctions and commended the role of MAIC in providing medical assistance to sick children in hospitals. The event raised considerable funds, which sponsored equipment for the Basrah Hospital and medicines and surgical items for other paediatric hospitals in Baghdad and its surroundings.

During 2002, MAIC members decided to hold several smaller fundraising events instead of the charity's annual dinner, which were also very rewarding.

On 11 June 2003, following the second Gulf War, MAIC held an Emergency War Relief Fund (EWRF), instead of its annual dinner. The event took place at the Royal College of Physicians, London. The panel included highly esteemed professional speakers: Dr Karol Sikora, Professor of Cancer Medicine at the Imperial College, Mr Peter Troy, the Humanitarian Programme Manager at the UK Department of International Development, and Ms Rym Brahimi, Middle East Correspondent at CNN, (known at present as HRH Princess Rym Ali Al-Hussein). The panel assessed the effects of the war on the health of children and addressed especially the rise of cancers among them.

The proceeds raised from the EWRF helped finance a relatively large emergency medical consignment which was made up of the items urgently needed by Iraqi paediatric hospitals following the war.

On 24 March 2004, we held our annual dinner at the Park Lane Hotel, London. We were privileged to have the Honourable Ms Claire Short MP as our guest speaker. Ms Short, who had resigned her post as Minister of International Development after the 2003 war, gave a keynote speech about the suffering of Iraqi children and praised MAIC's humanitarian aid.

On 19 November 2005, MAIC celebrated its humanitarian achievements at the Grosvenor House Hotel, London under the patronage of the late Dame Zaha Hadid, the Iraqi–British architect who was the first woman to receive the Pulitzer Architecture prize in 2004 and later the Sterling Prize in 2010 and 2011 consecutively. We were most honoured to have her support. Dame Zaha gave a very nostalgic commentary on Iraq; she spoke of her happy childhood memories of her country of birth and questioned the calamity that had befallen the children in Iraq following the UN sanctions and the two Gulf wars.

During 2006 and 2007, MAIC held several successful small fundraising functions which led the charity members to postpone the annual dinner for two consecutive years. Moreover, there was during this period, a notable increase in fundraising activities by non MAIC members who were supporters of the charity's humanitarian projects.

On 15 March 2008, MAIC held its last annual dinner at the Mandarin Oriental Hotel, London. We were very grateful to Miss Dina Mousawi, a young Iraqi actress, who donated her performance of a most captivating contemporary dance. The evening commemorated MAIC's humanitarian achievements over the past years and raised substantial funds for our last medical projects between 2008 and 2009.

Late Nizar Kabbani, the renowned Arab poet at MAIC's Poetry Recital at the Royal Geographical Society. London, 16 January 1996.

May and Mazin Al-Daftari congratulating Layla Pachachi, the mezzo soprano who donated her performance, and her accompanying pianist at MAIC's Annual Dinner. Dorchester, London, 18 June 1997.

Late Mr Robert Fisk, the renowned journalist, was the guest speaker at MAIC's Annual Dinner at The Dorchester Hotel. London, 27 May 1998.

Mr George Galloway (MP for Glasgow and Kelvin at the time)
was the guest speaker at MAIC's Annual Dinner at The Dorchester
Hotel. London, 27 May 1999.

Her Majesty Queen Rania Al-Abdullah of Jordan, Royal Patron and guest speaker at MAIC's Annual Dinner, surrounded by the charity members. The Brewery, London, 9 May 2001.

MAIC's event "Emergency War Relief Fund" (EWRF) at the Royal College of Physicians. The panel from right to left: Mr Peter Troy, Department of International Development, Dr Karol Sikora, Professor of Cancer Medicine at Imperial College, and Ms Rym Brahimi, at the time Middle East Correspondent at CNN and currently known as HRH Princess Rym Ali Al-Hussein.
The moderators on the far left and far right of the panel: Fatima Sheikh Khazaal, Trustee, and May Al-Daftari, Trustee and Chairman. London, 11 June 2003.

The Right Honourable Claire Short, MP, in conversation with Latifa Kosta, member of MAIC Board of Governors, and May Al-Daftari, Trustee and Chairman. Ms Short was the guest speaker at the Charity's Annual Dinner at the Park Lane Hotel. London, 24 March 2004.

Late Dame Zaha Hadid, the renowned world architect, was the guest speaker at MAIC's Annual Dinner at the Grosvenor House Hotel. London, 19 November 2005.

A group photo of MAIC members during the charity's last Annual Dinner with Ms Dina Mousawi, the young Iraqi modern dancer (third from the right) who donated her performance to the charity. The Mandarin Oriental Hotel. London, March 2008.

Chapter 8
MAIC Members in London and Amman

It is important to introduce and give deserving credit to MAIC members for their compassion in helping the children in Iraq and for the relentless voluntary work they offered the charity.

This chapter is about MAIC members at the London office and the Jordanian Liaison Committee. The role of the Medical Team in Iraq has already been discussed in Chapter 5.

MAIC Members in London

The London office was where all decisions were made. It included among its other responsibilities, the vetting of Iraqi hospital needs, planning fund raising events to purchase medical supplies, applying for UN approvals and export licences and arranging shipment of the supplies.

In the early days, all work was done from home by the Board of Governors, which included three Trustees – Professor Soad Tabaqchali, Sabah Mahmoud and myself – and seven other members: Dr Raghdah Shukri, Dr Kate Costelloe, Randa Smadi, Dr Nabil Al-Yaqubi, Salma Sambar, Haifa Al-Kaylani and Doris Riachy.

Secretarial work was done voluntarily, first by Muna Clark and then by May Achour, who later joined the Board of Governors.

After a few years, as the administrative work needed a larger space, we moved to office premises and employed one paid secretary. By that time, although some Board members had resigned, new ones joined, which increased its members to sixteen, including the six Trustees. The general work of the charity was carried out by the Board members, yet each of us became involved with specific responsibilities. Sabah Mahmoud (Trustee) dealt with legal and financial issues, and the late Robert Mabro, CBE (Trustee) with the general outlook and advice. Fatima Khazaal (Trustee), oversaw banking and events, while Hani Dajani (Trustee), took responsibility for checking prices of medical items and supervising supplies before dispatch. Doris Riachy (Trustee), also helped with charity events, as well as checking consignments at the warehouse. The rest of the Board members were very active in administration and fundraising activities. They chose venues, arranged the programmes for each evening and supervised the events. A significant part of the funds came from the hard work and dedication of the members, especially Salma Sambar, Latifa Kosta and Dunia Farman-Farmaian, who were very much involved in organising MAIC's annual dinners. In addition to my responsibilities as a Trustee and Chairman of the charity, I was in continuous contact with the doctors in Iraq, researching their most urgent requirements and visiting hospitals in Iraq. I also filled in the DTI applications, listing the medicines and the medical and surgical equipment which were needed and followed up the process of the UN approvals. Dr Hassan Haddad, another Board member, also provided us with lists of the items hospitals most urgently needed following his visits to Iraq.

The younger members of the Board of Governors, Joan Khan, May Achour, Dana Saadawi, Maysa Ibrahim, Maya Al-Memar, Rula Chorbachi and Bassam Zako, were very active in helping with the organisation of the fundraising events. They also handled with great efficiency MAIC's website and the production of the charity's yearly Newsletters.

The Honorary members were very supportive of MAIC's humanitarian work and offered all possible help and advice whenever it was needed. To name a few, Lady Beaumont, Dr Graham Walker and Dr Bruce Mathalone. Some members were also very active in organising fundraising events and donations, especially Tamima Ismail, Randa Smadi, Isaf Tayeb, Claira Habba and Najwa Jafar.

The young Support Committee, made up of Maya Askari, Sara Tayeb, Suha Najjar, Sabia Mayassi and Shereen Garbawi, offered much-needed help with great efficiency.

By 2009 MAIC's members totalled forty-seven. Everyone worked with strong determination and compassion towards the same humanitarian objective.

The Jordanian Liaison Committee

The Jordanian Liaison Committee was the link that facilitated the transfer of MAIC's medical supplies from London to Baghdad. Its members included Dr Junaid Mahmoud, Odette Atallah, Dr Mohamed Al Farekh, Dr Layla Sharaf, who was also a member of the Jordanian House of Lords, Dr Zafer Al Kayyali, Dr Salwan Baban, Hala Fattah and Zeina Shukri. They were passionate about the charity's humanitarian cause and were very eager to help.

I regularly met with the committee members at the homes of Odette and Layla as I passed through Amman on my way to Baghdad. The warm hospitality of the hostesses and the enthusiasm shown by the members for helping with the charity's work was remarkable. At the meetings, Hala Fattah usually briefed us about the custom clearance of MAIC's medical consignment in Amman and the process of its transport by land to Baghdad. We also discussed whether the driver and the escort had encountered any problems in passing through the customs point in Trabil or during the delivery of the supplies to our storage facility in the Medical City.

Between 2005 and 2008, when MAIC commenced offering Iraqi doctors short training programmes in UK hospitals, the Jordanian Liaison Committee, and in particular Dr Junaid Mahmoud, who was the core of the committee in Jordan, also played a vital role in organising the travel of these doctors, meeting the doctors on their arrival from Iraq, and providing them with visas, air tickets and expenses. The committee also arranged their accommodation and looked after them until the date of their travel to London.

These wonderful MAIC members in London, Amman and Baghdad (discussed in a previous chapter) together made the backbone of MAIC. What made the charity succeed in delivering humanitarian aid was the dedication and determination of these members to save as many vulnerable children as possible, no matter how difficult the circumstances were.

A group photo of MAIC members during the charity's "Iftar Meal" at Noura Restaurant. London, 7 November 2003.

A group photo of MAIC members at the Charity's Annual Dinner at Park Lane Hotel. London, 24 March 2004.

Chapter 9
Recollections

In including the following short narratives, I have endeavoured to highlight certain cherished experiences that affected me deeply. They are related to my involvement with MAIC in more ways than one. I have also included an insight into my new life in Amman, to complete the chain of the cities that I have lived in. My early years were in Baghdad, then I lived in Beirut and London and now Amman.

My First Land Journey to Baghdad

Since the summer of 1993, when I had last seen my mother in Amman, her health had rapidly deteriorated and she had become bedridden. The need to visit her in Baghdad and see the family and my home country after the Gulf War was weighing heavily on my conscience. I had planned this visit several times before, but on each occasion, I failed to follow it through. The idea of crossing the long lonely desert road terrified me, as I suffer from claustrophobia and agoraphobia. I lived with this emotional guilt for three years. Another factor that also pressed me to undertake this trip was my new responsibility as Chairman of MAIC; I knew it would be helpful for me to go in person to visit hospitals, find out about the health condition of children and meet the charity's appointed doctors.

On 14 January 1996 I learned that my good friends Samira and Fadil Rassoul Ali were going to Baghdad on 20 January. I was offered the chance to travel with them and immediately made up my mind to join them. I felt it would be my last chance to see my mother, who was in a state of partial coma.

I flew from London to Amman on 19 January, and on arrival a strange feeling of serenity embodied me, which I had not experienced for a long time. All my anxieties disappeared and the thought of seeing my mother after such a long time helped me to go through the dreary desert journey and reach my destination. After checking in at the Intercontinental Hotel I went immediately to a supermarket to buy food and other items needed by my family in the dire conditions they were experiencing. I also stopped by a pharmacy to stock up on my mother's medical requisites.

I left for Baghdad the following morning at 4 am with my friends Samira and Fadil. We drove in two GMC cars, sitting together in one car, which was driven by a good reliable man called Khathair. The second car followed with our luggage, food and my mother's medical supplies.

We started the journey in bad weather conditions; during the first two hours we had severe fog with virtually no visibility. The road from Amman to Ruwaishid (the Jordanian border) is a narrow dual carriageway and quite dangerous. A large number of transport vehicles use it to travel to and from Saudi Arabia, Syria and Iraq. The journey to Ruwaishid took five hours. We cleared passport control and customs very quickly thanks to recommendations and the help of dear and wonderful Jordanian friends.

After a few kilometres we reached Trabil, at the Iraqi border. Foreign diplomats and charity officials were usually taken to a VIP lounge, which was basic and clean. As I was representing the charity Medical Aid for Iraqi Children, I was welcomed with my friends and we were taken to the lounge, where we cleared passport control, customs and the HIV test, which was obligatory. The road from Trabil to Baghdad was very impressive, a smooth-running highway, with three lanes on each side surrounded by a desert of pink sand. We started our long drive through the Iraqi desert in bright sunshine, followed by a most picturesque sunset. As evening fell, I noticed how clear the sky was and how brilliant the stars were. We were able to see clearly the formation of the small bear and the larger bear. It brought back childhood memories of summer nights in Baghdad, sleeping on our roof terrace. I was always fascinated by the different star formations and would follow my favourite stars until I finally fell asleep.

It was 7 pm when I finally arrived home and went straight to my mother's room. I will never forget the moment I saw my mother and the expression of surprise and elation on her face. We could not stop embracing each other and crying. It was a painful emotional reunion with her and the rest of my family. I will always remember this long-awaited journey with mixed feelings of beauty, nostalgia and deep emotions, despite the fact that the road was dangerous, monotonous and exhausting.

I wrote the above account the day after my arrival in Baghdad on 20 January 1996. Since then, the highway between Trabil and Baghdad has become dilapidated and sections of the side rails have been looted, which has made it prone to fatal accidents. Sadly, our good driver Khathair, who drove me to Baghdad several times before 2002, died a few years later, when his car turned over on this same highway.

Living in Umnjasa

While we were living in London, one winter day, I remembered how Mazin and I started considering the idea of having a second home in a warmer climate. We had grown fond of Amman and its people during our frequent past visits to the country. Amman had become the place we met with our families during the Gulf wars and the sanction years.

We eventually built our dream home in Umnjasa in the outskirts of Amman and started to spend the cold winter months there since 2008. Although the area we have chosen to live in, outside of Amman, where we are surrounded by beautiful green fields and pink mountains, is peaceful and relaxing, we have had to accept its shortcomings. The most serious one was not having internet lines during the first few years of our settlement. Thank God, the iPhone did work. I used it for my urgent messages and emails. Otherwise, I went to internet cafes in town to do more serious work. In 2015, we were able to install Wi-Fi, which greatly improved our internet communications.

Another shortcoming of our location is that we have poor landlines. Besides, once in a while one or more of our telephone land lines get cut off due to worn-out wires and sometimes even stolen cables. It seems cables are valuable for their copper content.

Although it might seem strange, despite feeling distant and cut off at times, the beauty of the place and the serenity surrounding us make it worth living where we are and compensate for any feeling of disconnection.

A Conversation with My Granddaughter

In April 2010, our daughter Lara with her husband Jihad Tabbara and their four daughters Rhea, Talia, Tara and little Darya came to spend the Easter break with us in Amman and to enjoy outdoor activities, swim at our lap pool and visit the famous archaeological sites in Jordan.

During their stay, we visited Ma'in and spent the day at the hot springs. It was a wonderful experience, swimming under a waterfall where the water temperature is about 65 degrees. One evening I spent quality time with my granddaughter Talia, who was fifteen years old. I showed her the notes she wrote when she was eight. She had been deeply affected by the daily news on television covering the preparations for the second Gulf War and the effect of sanctions on little children. She wrote in French as she was studying at a French school in Monaco.

Her notes were short but revealed a deep sense of observation and sensitivity uncommon in a child as young as she was. In her first note she wrote, 'I wonder why people fight wars, it is a pity. If only people thought of the others who suffer.' A few weeks later, she wrote, 'They should not kill innocent people just because of one man. I hope President Bush can see how people have nothing to eat.' When she was nearly nine, she with two of her friends raised money for MAIC by circulating a note she had written: 'If all the world gives a little bit of money you will see how the world will be more beautiful and there will be less unhappy people suffering because they do not have enough money to eat, pay doctors and buy their medicines etc.... In countries where there is a war now or in the past, think if you were in their place. And thank you to the people who gave, it is very generous.'

As we read her notes, tears were rolling from Talia's eyes and I remembered how emotional I was when I first read them and decided to keep the notes as a souvenir for her.

Unforgettable Massacre

On 3 March 2010, one of the ugliest kinds of human behaviour took place in Baghdad, Christians were massacred at Saydat Al-Najat Church. Over fifty worshippers, including two priests, were shot and killed and scores were injured following the raid on the church. It was a most appalling act of barbarism, and could not have been imagined a decade before.

As I watched the news on television, I remembered the visit I made with Fatima on 2 May 2004 to the church of St Chad in Sunderland. I will always treasure the memories of the visit; meeting Reverend John Stephenson, talking to the caring and compassionate congregation and giving the Sunday sermon. I remembered how I spoke to them about the brotherly relations between Christians and Muslims and how they had lived together side by side as one community over the past centuries.

Six years had passed since that visit and how could I explain to those wonderful people at St Chad what had happened at Saydat Al-Najat Church in Baghdad, Iraq? Could I say that the values of the people I knew so well had changed? Do wars change people's convictions and behaviour? I felt a terrible sense of grief and disbelief.

What we see today in the new "Democratic Iraq" is a fragmented society which has lost its most essential human codes. The breakdown in security and the eruption of violence following the 2003 war unfortunately led to political and sectarian killing between Shiites and Sunnis and escalated as well to the killing of innocent Christians.

Ten days later, on the evening of 13 November, I joined a mass at the Catholic Church in Windsor Way, London, in remembrance of all who died in the massacre at Saydat Al-Najat. The Church was packed with people. As the priest called the names of the perished children, women and men, people cried and sobbed. We were all feeling the pain and our voices joined together, condemning this cowardly act. The strong message of the speaker was to call on Iraqis to protect their Christian brothers and assure them of their safety. He also pleaded with them not to leave their country. Christians are an important part of Iraq's population and share with Muslims the country's history.

Nostalgia

Unlike the usual warm and sunny October weather in Amman, it was a rainy and foggy morning and I was on my way to a yoga class at the gym centre, "One with Life". The half-hour drive from home to the centre in Amman was a good time to reflect. I often go back in my thoughts to certain passed episodes. The weather that day reminded me of my land trips to Baghdad, when I used to travel early in the morning, around 4 o'clock, when it was still dark and cold. On that October day I felt a special nostalgia to see the little faces of the young cancer patients we used to treat and was anxious to know if they had been provided with their treatment. I also missed the letters I used to receive from our doctors, Khalid Al Obaydi, Mazen Al Jaidry, Jawad Al Ali and Hussein Malik, listing the urgent needs of their hospitals. I deeply missed all the wonderful professional relationships we had established over so many years.

As I remembered the many happy drawing competitions organised by the Said Foundation (formerly KRSF), it brought back a sad memory of a little girl who was four years old and had leukaemia. She won a prize, but by the time we were able to send her gift box to the hospital, she was unfortunately dead. I could not hold back my tears as I read Dr Jaidry's letter stating that her gift was handed over to her sister as the little girl had already passed away.

Invitation to Munich

One of the experiences that made a special impression on me was attending Le Cercle meeting in Munich, which was held between 7 and 10 June 2001. I was invited as one of several speakers by the RT Honourable Lord Lamont, who was the chairman of Le Cercle at the time. The meeting is usually held twice a year. Europeans and Americans, such as MPs, members of the House of Lords, diplomats, members of the armed forces, lawyers and businessmen are invited to exchange views on world affairs.

I was invited to talk about the implications of the sanctions which were imposed on Iraq in 1990 and their effects on the people of Iraq. I hesitated at first, as the majority of attendees would be high-ranking political and military male officials. Moreover, the political atmosphere at the time was in favour of building a consensus for a war on Iraq. I wondered how I, a female representing a small humanitarian charity to help Iraqi children, could address such a crowd! After giving it some thought, however, I accepted the invitation and stressed that my talk would address the effects of sanctions only from a humanitarian perspective. I also expressed my wish not to be drawn into a political debate.

After my arrival on 7 June and during the get-together evening gathering, I felt a little uneasy and nervous. As my talk was scheduled for 9 June, I had more time over the next day to meet with and talk to some of the participants during lunch, coffee breaks and dinner. Some asked me about the contents of my talk; others tried to provoke me with satirical questions such as what I thought about the atrocities of the Iraqi regime and whether I had met Saddam Hussein. I kept calm and explained that I represented a humanitarian British charity that offered medical aid to children's hospitals and that it had nothing to do with the regime in Iraq or its president. I also told them that I never met with government officials or Saddam Hussein during my visits to Iraq. I gave examples of heartbreaking stories of little children who were in desperate need of unavailable medicines. Gradually, I felt that some of the participants started to sympathise with the charity's cause and listened with interest to my stories.

When it was time for me to go to the podium and deliver my talk, entitled "Can Sanctions against Iraq be Justified?", some of the participants who were seated close by had become more sympathetic and wished me good luck. My address was well-received and had a good round of applause.

During the few minutes of questions and answers, I had interesting and relevant questions which I was happy to answer, but when questions became more political, the moderator intervened and refused them. Of course, I was expecting some of the audience not to be in agreement with my presentation. Hence I was not surprised when one elderly man came rushing up to me during the break and said, 'You know what, all this suffering that you talked about; they deserve it!' He turned his back and left before I could answer.

It was very interesting to listen to other speakers, who covered a variety of topics concerning European countries, African nations, Atlantic Alliance relations, security issues, foreign policy and defence systems. I was glad that I did participate and hoped that my talk had a positive influence on some of the audience and made them realise how sanctions had catastrophic effects on a nation and caused unprecedented suffering on innocent people and especially children.

The last paragraph of my address summarised my message:

'I represent a humanitarian, non-political charity and I am not necessarily in a position to judge the political merits of the sanctions policy. Nevertheless, as a humanitarian, I believe no matter what the political gains may have been, they could not have justified this scale of human tragedy.'

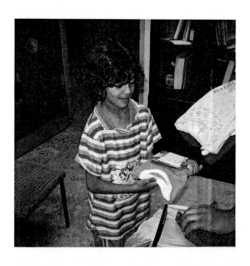

A seven-year-old girl receiving a gift box on behalf of her younger sister, who won the Said Foundation drawing competition, but sadly died of Leukaemia before receiving the gift prize.

Dr Mazin Al Jadiry, oncologist and a member of MAIC medical team, handing over the said gift prize to the young seven-year-old girl. Al Mansour Paediatric Teaching Hospital, Baghdad, 2005.

Epilogue

This book examines the years that led to the formation of MAIC through my personal life experience.

It then reviews the sanction resolutions on Iraq from the time they were adopted in August 1990, the subsequent reviews that followed, of which the "Oil-for-Food Programme" was the most significant and finally the lifting of the sanctions in May 2003. The adoption of "Comprehensive" sanctions was unique to Iraq and it meant that all imports to and exports from Iraq were totally prohibited. They caused unparalleled damage to the health of Iraqis, especially children. The book also covers the many problems faced by MAIC in dealing with different sanctions departments while seeking permission to export the charity's medical consignments to Iraq. It also commends the role of Iraqi doctors in coping with scarce medical resources during those challenging years.

The book also describes briefly the health conditions and education standards in Iraq prior to 1990, when medical standards and education were among the best in the Middle East. In fact, health care was available freely in the whole country. Education was compulsory among citizens and Iraq was honoured by UNESCO for its promotion of education for all.

Children, being the most vulnerable sector of society, were the main focus of the charity. The book highlights the effects of sanctions on them. Observations compiled from MAIC members and statistics quoted from reports published by international humanitarian organisations such as UNICEF, WHO and WFP paint a disturbing picture of the health of children. These conservative statistics estimated that 560,000 children died from hunger and disease between 1990 and 1995, 800,000 under five suffered from chronic malnutrition by 2000, and two million others suffered from protein-, calorie- and vitamin-related malnutrition in 1998.

The book also examines the trauma the children underwent as a result of having lived in a war zone and the conflict situations which followed the second Gulf War. Such a horrifying environment meant that many of them suffered from enormous psychological disorders as well as from disabling injuries.

Throughout fourteen years of my chairmanship of MAIC, I witnessed the pain and suffering of these children as the sanctions and wars tightened their grip on them. With my colleagues at MAIC and the help of thousands of donors we did our best to save and help as many children as possible. The passionate and tireless work exerted by MAIC members and the selfless efforts made by donors and supporters in raising funds to achieve the charity's humanitarian goals have been precisely highlighted.

It is 2020 and over ten years since the winding up of MAIC. The children we took care of and hopefully saved will have grown up into adulthood. They represent a small but significant, sample of millions of young adults who were born and grew up in dire conditions as a result of sanctions through the two Gulf wars. It is sad to say it is a generation made of a few million who suffered tragically from malnutrition, disease, injuries, wounds, psychological disorders and handicaps that maimed them for ever. Included in this generation are millions who were orphaned and grew up in meagre circumstances. Education, which is the basis of teaching and building a nation was substantially degraded because of a lack of books, teaching facilities and aids. Schools were dilapidated and classrooms, if they existed, were poorly equipped and were unhealthily damp with leaking ceilings and broken windows.

Now I look back and wonder what was this generation of young adults could possibly have done wrong to have had to face such cruel measures which deprived them of food, medical care and education in their innocent childhood years? Their suffering was manmade and could have been prevented.

The millions of adults over the age of twenty-five who survived this tragedy could have been part of the valuable Iraqi workforce, or the builders of a new democratic Iraq. Instead they are weak, and in desperate need of assistance. Their basic human rights have been violated and urgently need to be addressed by the international community which was responsible in the first place for their plight.

Over the past few years, we have witnessed many debates about the validity of the elongated sanctions imposed on Iraq that had resulted in the loss of millions of lives and inflicted unprecedented suffering on the population.

Do the countries at the UN, who were responsible for passing these crippling resolutions which affected the most vulnerable of Iraqis, feel any responsibility and remorse?

Surprisingly, the world is silent in the face of this tragedy. Has the world lost its humanity?

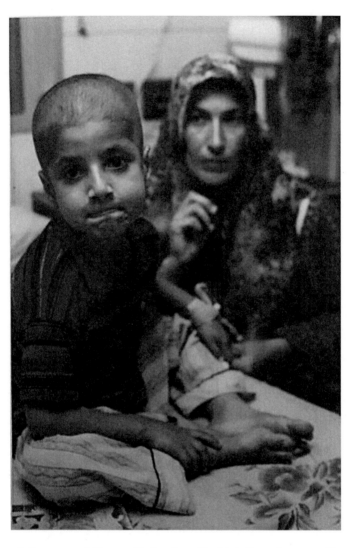

A four-year-old boy suffering from Burkitt's Lymphoma at Al Mansour Paediatric Teaching Hospital. Baghdad, September 2000.

Appendices

Charity Lunch

in benefit of
the International Committee of the Red Cross Activities
to Relieve Famine and Disease in Iraq

with a little help...

19 October 1991
Grosvenor House
Park Lane London

Appendix 1: Fundraising Lunch to Benefit ICRC's Project to
Repair Water Plants in Iraq, October 1991

A BRIEF BACKGROUND ON MAIC

The decision to establish the Charity, Medical Aid for Iraqi Children (MAIC), was taken in 1994, as a result of the rapidly deteriorating health and nutritional conditions of Iraqi children since 1991.

As the concern to help the children became paramount, a group of the present Board of Governors took the decision to form the Charity and help save as many of the children as possible. MAIC was registered as a British Charity in February 1995.

MAIC operates through a Board of Governors in London and coordinates with a Liaison Committee in Amman and a Medical Team in Iraq.

MAIC's primary role is to provide urgently needed medical supplies to paediatric hospitals in Iraq. The Charity also aims to treat Iraqi children with complicated medical needs in Amman or elsewhere.

LATEST STATISTICS FROM THE UN ORGANISATIONS

According to a report prepared by UNICEF, the World Health Organisation and the World Food Programme (WFP) published in June 1995, 23% of Iraqi Children below the age of 5 are suffering from malnutrition.

The same report sites malnutrition as being responsible for 39% of Child Mortality - a level that, in real terms, has reached 11,000 children monthly.

In a distressing comment on the conditions of the children in Iraq the WFP described the effect of malnutrition as causing irreparable damage for a whole generation of children, whose condition has been described as irreversible.

According to another recent report by the Food and Agriculture Organisation (FAO) more than 560,000 children have died since 1991.

If you wish to make a contribution, kindly fill in the contribution slip and return it with your donation to the address below.

-------- ✂ --------

MAIC
CONTRIBUTION SLIP
Registered Charity No. 1044222

I would like to make a donation of £.............................
Cheques made payable to **Medical Aid for Iraqi Children.**

Name:

Address:

                                     Postcode:
Please indicate if a receipt is required.

Medical Aid for Iraqi Children
Attention: Mr Sabah Mahmoud
Carmelite House, 50 Victoria Embankment,
Blackfriars, London EC4Y 0DX

Appendix 2: The Charity Members, from MAIC's Newsletter, 1995

HOW TO DONATE

Please note that Medical Aid for Iraqi Children is winding up on 30th June 2009. Donations will be accepted until 31st March 2009.

BY CHEQUE

I would like to make a donation of
Please make cheques payable to **MAIC**

Name:
Address:

Postcode: Country:

Please request a receipt if required and
advise your forwarding address

BY CREDIT OR DEBIT CARDS ONLINE
Please make your credit or debit card donations online by using our secure facility at
www.justgiving.com/maic/donate

BY BANKERS DRAFT
Beneficiary MAIC:

Bank Duncan Lawrie Limited
1 Hobart Place
London SW1W OHU
Telephone: 020 7245 1234
Fax: 020 7245 6276

US$ account number: 78532040
GBP account number: 08532030
Euro account number: 58532030
Sort Code: 60-93-77

BY CAF
For CAF card holders, please quote in full:
Medical Aid for Iraqi Children

MAIC
26 Old Brompton Road, London SW7 3DL England
Tel: 020 7581 2727   Fax: 020 7581 2767
e.mail: info@maic.org.uk   website: www.maic.org.uk
Registered Charity No. 1044222

Appendix 3: The Charity Members, from MAIC's Newsletter, 2008

Children's Welfare Hospital, Medical City, Baghdad (previously Al- Mansour Paediatric Teaching Hospital)

Central Paediatric Teaching Hospital, Al Tifl Al- Markazi, Baghdad

Basrah Paediatric Hospotal, Basrah

Ninewah/ Mosul Paediatric Teaching Hospital, Mosul

Al- Karamah Hospital, Baghdad

Al- Jamhouria Hospital, Basrah

Diwania Teaching Hospital, Diwania

Abdul Kadir Mahmoud Charitable Medical Clinic, Mosul

Kerbala Children's Hospital, Kerbala

Ibn Baladi Paediatric Hospital, Baghdad

Al- Alwiyah Children's Hospital, Baghdad

Kadisya General Hospital, Paediatric Section, Baghdad

Kirkuk General Hospital, Paediatric Section, Kirkuk

Al- Habibia for Children, Baghdad

Samawa Children and Obstetric Hospital, Samawa

Al- Furat Al- Awsat , South of Iraq

Ramadi Hospital Paediatric Section, A- Anbar

Dar Al- Tamrith, Neonate Department, Baghdad

Central Paediatric Teaching Hospital, Neonate Department, Baghdad

Al- Nasria Hospital, South of Iraq

Amara Hospital, South of Iraq

Al- Kadhmiah Hospital, Baghdad

Appendix 4: Receiving Hospitals and Medical Centres Between 1995 and 2009

Hilla Hospital, Hilla

Spinal Cord Injury Centre, Baghdad

Basrah Women and Children's Hospital, Basrah

Mousl Blood Bank Mosul

Falluja General Hospital, Falluja

Basrah Prosthetic Centre, Basrah

Al- Wasiti Hospital, Baghdad

Iraqi Human Relief Organisation, Baghdad

Miscellaneous medical items were donated during the earlier years of MAIC; to visiting European team of doctors carrying free heart operations on children and also items for bon marrow transplantation.

Annex(I:AF) - Application Form for authorisation to supply to Iraq

SECURITY COUNCIL COMMITTEE ESTABLISHED BY RESOLUTION 661 (1990)
CONCERNING THE SITUATION BETWEEN IRAQ AND KUWAIT
NOTIFICATION OR REQUEST TO SHIP GOODS TO IRAQ

(TO BE COMPLETED BY THE SECRETARIAT)

COMM No   REGISTRATION DATE   DEADLINE FOR OBJECTION

(TO BE COMPLETED BY PROSPECTIVE EXPORTING COUNTRY OR INT'L ORG)

1. MISSION OR INTERNATIONAL ORGANISATION   CERTIFYING SIGNATURE AND OFFICIAL SEAL

2. DATE OF SUBMISSION   3 MISSION REFERENCE NO

4a. Sector/item code (SCR986) 4b HS tariff code	5. GOODS TO BE SHIPPED (Name and/or description. Attach additional sheet if necessary)	6. QUANTITY IN NUMBERS	7. UNIT OF MEASUREMENT	8. VALUE PER ITEM	9. TOTAL VALUE	10. CURRENCY ISO CODE
1 a)						
b)						
2 a)						
b)						
3 a)						
b)						

11. EXPORTER Name and Address

12. ORIGIN of GOODS (if different from applicant State)

13. RECEIVING COMPANY / ORG Name and Address

14. SHIPPING ARRANGEMENTS
a) Border Point or Port of Entry into Iraq

b) Means of Transportation

c) Other Information (e.g. route, major ports, etc.)

□ From the Iraq Account in accordance with SC resolution 986 (1995) (relevant documentation including contract(s) must be attached)

15 METHOD OF PAYMENT

□ By other arrangement (Provide as many details as possible)

16. ADDITIONAL INFORMATION: End-use and End-user (Attach additional sheet if necessary)

IMPORTANT NOTICE

1 Provide only one item per line in Box 5.
2 Sector/item codes (Box 4a) are mandatory, and are found in the Annexes to the Distribution Plan of SCR 986.
3 HS Tariff Codes (Box 4b), if used, must be 6-digit codes of the International Harmonised System of Tariff Nomenclature as determined by the Customs Cooperation Council in Brussels, Belgium.
4 Information entered must match shipping documents presented to customs officials.
5 Incomplete, incorrect or illegible applications will be returned by the Committee's Secretariat for completion.

Appendix 5: A Sample of the UN Application Form and the DTI Guidance Note

ANNEX(I:AF) CONTD   MISSION REFERENCE No:

Additional sheet to notify or request to ship goods to:

4a. Sector/item code (SCR986) 4b HS tariff code	5. GOODS TO BE SHIPPED (Name and/or description. Attach additional sheet if necessary)	6. QUANTITY IN NUMBERS	7. UNIT OF MEASUREMENT	8. VALUE PER ITEM	9. TOTAL VALUE	10. CURRENCY ISO CODE
4 a)						
b)						
5 a)						
b)						
6 a)						
b)						
7 a)						
b)						
8 a)						
b)						
9 a)						
b)						
10a)						
b)						
11a)						
b)						
12a)						
b)						
13a)						
b)						
14a)						
b)						
15a)						
b)						
16a)						
b)						
17a)						
b)						
18a)						
b)						
19a)						
b)						
20a)						
b)						

Annex(I:AF) (UN Application Form): notes

The United Nations has issued this Application Form for applications for authorisation or for notification of the supply of goods to Iraq. Please note the following guide to completion of the form. Any form not correctly filled in may be returned to the applicant.

- **Language:** applications should be completed either in English or in French.

- **Presentation:** in black and preferably typewritten .

- **Boxes 4(a)** (only for SCR986) 5, 6, 7, 8, 9, 10, 11, 13, 14 and 15 must be completed by the applicant.

- **Box 4(a)** the sector/item codes are to be found in Iraq's Distribution Plan.

- **Boxes 4(b) and 16**, if completed, will assist processing procedures and facilitate the shipment of the goods.

- **Box 4 (HS Code);**
  - ◊ if used, should be limited to the first six digits of the harmonised system of the tariff.
  - ◊ one item or HS tariff code per line. One total weight and value per item or HS tariff code.
  - ◊ goods covered by the same HS code should be treated as one item; e.g. medicaments containing other antibiotics packed for retail sale, tariff heading 300420, should not be sub-divided by brand name.

- **Box 6 (Quantity)** should be given in whole numbers.

- **Box 7 (Units of Measurement)**
  - ◊ for liquids, use litres; for dry goods, use kilos or tons. Exceptions: items like shoes could use "pairs"; heavy items like pumps could use "pieces". Do not use "boxes", "cases", etc.

- **Box 8 (Value per Item);** where possible this should reflect the price of a single item; e.g. one lightbulb rather than a box or a kilo of lightbulbs.

- **Box 9 (Total Value)** should be given in whole numbers.

- **Box 10 (Currency)** should be given in full or abbreviated using the ISO code; e.g. GBP for Pounds Sterling.

- **Boxes 14(a) and (c)** must be completed for shipments made in connection with United Nations Security Council Resolution 986 (1995); and in other cases they should still be completed whenever the information is available.

- **Box 14(a)** (Border point or point of entry): only one may be cited per application. For supplies made in accordance with SCR 986, only Trebil, Zakho and Umm Qasr will be accepted.

- **Box 14(c)** (Other information); give the exporting country, plus details of the shipping arrangements (major ports) and any other relevant information relating to the shipping arrangements.

- **Box 15 (Method of Payment)** Tick one box.
  - ◊ if payment is requested from the Iraq Account in accordance with Security Council Resolution 986 (1995), the application must be accompanied by all relevant documentation, including the concluded contractual arrangements.
  - ◊ if marked "By other arrangement" and the arrangement is to be by Letter of Credit, the issuing bank and date of payment should be given if possible.

133

UNITED NATIONS · NATIONS UNIES

POSTAL ADDRESS ADRESSE POSTALE UNITED NATIONS, N.Y. 10017

CABLE ADDRESS ADRESSE TELEGRAPHIQUE UNATIONS NEWYORK

REFERENCE

SECURITY COUNCIL COMMITTEE ESTABLISHED BY RESOLUTION 661 (1990)
CONCERNING THE SITUATION BETWEEN IRAQ AND KUWAIT

S/AC.25/1999/661/OC.3612

12 October 1999
NOT VALID AFTER 9 APRIL 2000

Sir,

On behalf of the Security Council Committee established by resolution 661 (1990) concerning the situation between Iraq and Kuwait, I have the honour to acknowledge receipt of your communication dated 1 October 1999 (ref. QX/447/99) concerning the intended shipment to Iraq, as a donation, of specified quantities of humanitarian items, as indicated in your form. For security and inspection purposes, a copy of your communication is attached hereto.

I have the honour to inform you that, in accordance with the Committee's decision taken on 22 March 1991 (document S/22400), the members of the Committee have no objection to the sending of the specified items which fall within the category of materials and supplies for essential civilian needs referred to in paragraph 20 of Security Council resolution 687 (1991).

Further, I have the honour to suggest that your Government ensure that copies of this communication are provided to those engaged in the shipment of the specified items destined for Iraq.

This letter of approval will cease to be valid after 9 April 2000.

Accept, Sir, the assurances of my highest consideration.

A. Peter van Walsum
Chairman
Security Council Committee established
by resolution 661 (1990) concerning the
the situation between Iraq and Kuwait

His Excellency
Mr. Stewart Eldon
Ambassador
Deputy Permanent Representative of the United Kingdom
to the United Nations

DTI
25-10-99
APPROVED

Appendix 6: UN Letter of Authorization to the DTI

Dr May Al-Daftari
Medical Aid for Iraqi Children
26 Old Brompton Road
London
SW7 3DL

**Department of
Trade and Industry**

Kingsgate House
66-74 Victoria Street
London SW1E 6SW

General enquiries
0171 215 5000
Textphone:
0171 215 6740

Direct line 0171 215 8094
Direct fax 0171 215 8386
Our ref QX/447/99
Your ref
Date ⁊₀October 1999

Dear Dr Al-Daftari,

UN SANCTIONS AGAINST IRAQ: EXPORT LICENCE

I enclose the export licence QX/447/99 permitting you to export the goods listed in the Schedule to the Licence from the United Kingdom to Iraq. **The Licence is valid up to and including 9th April 2000.** I also enclose a copy of the United Nations letter (number S/AC.25/1999/661/OC.3612, of 12th October 1999) which confirms the UN Sanctions Committee's approval for this supply of goods. A copy of this Letter should accompany the goods to the point of entry into Iraq.

You are reminded that UN Sanctions in respect of trade with Iraq, and legislation implementing them, remain in force. Accordingly, you need to consider carefully whether any action relating to Iraq is prohibited or requires a licence from this Department. You should also note that this licence does not guarantee payment. **If in any doubt on this or any other point please get in touch with me at the address or telephone number at the head of this letter.**

Yours sincerely

A Smith
Ms A Smith

p:\msoff43\winword\template\pletterd.dot

dti
Department of Trade and Industry

Appendix 7: Export Licence to MAIC Issued by the DTI

QX/447/99

EXPORT LICENCE

AS

THIS LICENCE IS NOT TRANSFERABLE OR ASSIGNABLE

The Secretary of State, in exercise of powers conferred by Article 3 of the Export of Goods (Control) (Iraq and Kuwait Sanctions) Order 1990 (a) ("the Exports Order"), hereby grants the following Licence:

1.   Subject to the following provisions of this Licence, **MEDICAL AID FOR IRAQI CHILDREN** is authorised to export the goods specified in the Schedule hereto from the United Kingdom or the Isle of Man to any destination in Iraq or to any destination in any other country for delivery, directly or indirectly, to a person for the purposes of any business carried on in or operated from Iraq.

2.   This Licence must be produced to the proper officer of HM Customs and Excise with the shipping documents when the goods are presented to him or her for exportation unless that officer allows otherwise.

3.   The authorization in paragraph 1 is subject to the condition that written notice shall be given within 14 days of exportation to the Secretary of State of the following particulars:-
     (a)   date of exportation;
     (b)   method and route of transport from the United Kingdom to the destination including flag-vessel;
     (c)   confirmation of the value of the goods at the date of exportation.

4.   Nothing in this Licence shall affect any prohibition or restriction on the exportation of any goods under or by virtue of any enactment, other than a prohibition or restriction in the Exports Order or the Iraq and Kuwait (United Nations Sanctions) Order 1990 (b).

5.   Any expression used in this Licence shall have the meaning it has in the Exports Order or the Import, Export and Customs Powers (Defence) Act 1939 (c).

6.   This Licence shall come into force forthwith.

7.   This Licence is valid up to and including 9th April 2000.

8.   This Licence shall not be assigned or otherwise transferred.

For and on behalf of the   A Smith   25th   October 1999
Secretary of State   ASMITH
Department of Trade and Industry   AS

WARNING: Failure to comply with the provisions of this Licence may lead to forfeiture of the goods or to prosecution.

NOTE: This Licence may be modified or revoked at any time by the Secretary of State.

(a) S.I. 1990/1640
(b) S.I. 1990/1651, as amended
(c) 1939 c.69.

DTI
25-10-99 AS
APPROVED

Echo
International
Health
Services
Limited

Registered Office
**Ullswater Crescent
Coulsdon Surrey CR5 2HR**
Telephone
081-660 2220
Telex No   Fax No
924507 ECHO G   081-668 0751

Company No 1039894 (England)
Registered in the UK as a Charity No 294891
VAT Registration No G8216063690

President
Surgeon Vice Admiral Sir James Watt KBE

Chairman
F. W. P. (Bill) Bentley MA

Chief Executive
Keith W. Slater FCA

Medical Director
John Townsend FRCS

Our ref: SS/MM

Your ref: ST/ST8888

Professor Tabaqchali
Kent Terrace
Regents Park
London
NW1 4RP

17th October 1995

Dear Professor Tabaqchali

Ref: IQ/251337 - 251268
(Previous IQ/250607/608/609 & 250435)

Further to our telephone conversation the situation is as follows:
The supplier Vickers has been blocked by an unhelpful US Treasury in the processing
of the licence application, to the extent that death threats have been received
by workers at Vickers.

One of Vickers UK staff is travelling out to the US this week and shall request
an audience/meeting with the person responsible for issuing the US licence. The
embargo of goods to various countries have a "humanitarian" clause, which should
be applicable in this case. If this is fruitless, a decision shall be made by
Vickers as a company whether to ship the goods anyway or cancel the order and assist
in finding a suitable alternative. Although this process has taken some time to
date , it is thought likely that the goods shall be supplied. The personal represen-
tation should produce results and we should be apprised of these quite soon.

As any further information is received, we shall inform you directly.

Yours sincerely

SPScH

Susan P Scott RGN

Appendix 8: ECHO's Letter to MAIC Regarding the Blockage of
the Export License to Vicker Incubators, 17 October 1995

THE PLIGHT OF ACADEMICS IN IRAQ

The plight of Academics in Iraq is an extract from a talk given by Dr. Abdul Karim Alobedy MD at University College London. Dr. Alobedy is the Chairman of the Iraqi Association for Child Mental Health (IACMH) and is a Consultant Psychiatrist at Al-Yarmouk Teaching Hospital.

The health care system in Iraq continues to encounter a shortage of staff, equipment and medicines as well as sporadic electricity and water supplies. All hospital buildings and almost 90% of health centers require repair or total reconstruction (Dahr Jamail, June 2005 & UNHCR COI report, Oct. 2005). Between April 2003 and May 2006 more than 106 doctors were killed, 164 nurses were killed and 77 wounded, 142 non-medical staff were killed and 117 wounded. In the past two years 250-300 Iraqi doctors have been kidnapped. In May 2006 eight doctors were killed and 42 wounded, 8 nurses were killed and 7 wounded, and of non-medical staff 6 were killed and 4 wounded. (The wounded individuals have high mortality due to lack of life-saving measures.) (UNAMI report June 2006 & HRW Oct.2005).

With escalating violence in Iraq since 2003, doctors are increasingly the victims of attacks and kidnappings for ransom by criminal gangs or by insurgents. As a result, doctors are fleeing Iraq. Roughly half of 34,000 Iraqi physicians registered with the Iraqi Medical Association have fled the country. More than 10% of Baghdad's total force of registered doctors left or were driven from work during the last year, a number which has risen sharply since early 2005. (Iraqi Medical Association (which licenses practitioners) 2006 & IRIN 18 Nov. 2006). An average of thirty doctors has fled the country each month since Oct. 2005 (HRW report Oct 2005). Furthermore, because of the proliferation of weapons, doctors and nurses face insecurity inside hospitals, kidnapping of their patients, pressure by militias and other armed forces and groups in order to sign certificates or to prioritize treatment. The threats are mainly addressed against senior doctors such as directors and head of departments, resulting in complex surgeries being handled by inexperienced staff or not performed at all

(UNAMI report June 2006). Hundred of private clinics have been closed in the capital Baghdad, after gangs started to kill doctors while they were attending to patients (IRIN 18 Nov.2006).

The mental health services are the worst part of the health care system in Iraq. (Medact July 2005). The number of people suffering with mental illness in Baghdad has risen since the 2003 war. Moreover the absence of acute psychiatric services, and consulting services, and a general lack of knowledge of psychiatric aspects of medical illness is a serious problem in a society that has endured years of political oppression, and suffers from a high level of poverty and violence (The MFP. 7 Feb.2005 & Daily Telegraph, 24 Jan, 2005). The brain drain in this field reached 73% of the most best qualified and experienced experts in Psychiatry, and it is 100% in Baghdad Medical College (Table 1).

Table 1: "The Brain Drain" of Professors and High Academics in Psychiatry.

Medical College	No. of Psychiatric Academics in 2003	No. of Psychiatric Academics in 2006	% of Brain Drain
Baghdad	6	0	100
Almustansyria	3	1	66.6
Al-Nahreen	2	1	50
Mosul	2	1	50
Basrah	2	1	50
Total	15	4	73

Over the past three years thousands of Iraq's finest minds have had to flee the flames engulfing Iraq. The tragedy engulfing Iraq is the systematic liquidation of the country's academics and professionals, which means the destruction of Iraq's cultural

4

Appendix 9: Extract- 'The Plight of Academicians in Iraq', by Karim Alobeydi, MAIC Newsletter, 2006

THE PLIGHT OF ACADEMICS IN IRAQ... cont.

identity. Targeting professors and doctors and depriving the country of its sharpest thinkers will destroy the higher education system in Iraq, which, in turn, will destroy other sectors of society by deterioration in the level of teaching and the provision of health services.

While 90% of Iraqi's are suffering from mental distress (study by one expert - Daily Telegraph 24 Jan. 2006), of the 100 Psychiatrists in Iraqi up to 2003, 50% of them now out of the country. The number of reconstructive surgeons in Iraq before the 2003 was 34, twenty of them have either been murdered or fled; 72% of Iraqis needing reconstructive surgery are suffering from gunshot or blast wounds. Easily treatable conditions such as diarrhoea and respirato-

ry illness caused 70% of all child deaths.
47 % children and adolescents in Baghdad report exposure to major traumatic events during the past 2 years. And 30% of the children and adolescents in Mosul had symptoms of post traumatic stress disorder - PTSD. (Razokhi, Lancet Sept. 2006). While, 50 % of children in Baghdad have conduct problems (Alobedy 2006); This in spite of the fact that there are no child psychiatric services in the country.

More than 90% of Iraqi University Academics have Death Anxieties of various kinds. (The essential task of the academic is to create life in its highest aims, beginning with lectures, scientific research, whether theoretical, or inside laboratories or in the field, and to accumulate eternal truths in enriching "the human mind library". Is it possible for such a creator of life to coexist with deep and objective anxiety of assassination and the fear of death?) (Professor of Psychology - Baghdad Oct. 2006).

Many wives and children of academics and professionals were murdered, and hundreds of their children were kidnapped . By targeting those who hold the keys to Iraq's reconstruction and development, the perpetrators of this violence are jeopardising the future of Iraq and democracy (UNESCO's director general 2006).

A four year old girl with Rhabdomyosarcoma at the Children's Welfare Hospital Baghdad, May 2006

A nine year old boy with Hodgkin's disease at the Children's Welfare Hospital Baghdad, May 2006

5

139

بسم الله الرحمن الرحيم

MINISTRY OF HEALTH
MEDICAL CITY
Baghdad - IRAQ

وزارة الصحـة
مؤسسة مدينة الطب
بغداد ــ العراق

No. :—
Date :— 22nd May 1997

Mrs. May Al-Daftari
M.A.I.C.

Dear Mrs. Al-Daftari,

Thank you for your letter of April 18th, 1997. As for your letter of Jan. 10th.97, the answer has been posted to you two weeks ago. The incubators which have been mentioned in your letter of Jan 31st have not benn received yet.

The last delivery of lactose free-milk and medical supplies have been used since delivery on 31st March 1997. After one month the expected duration of milk and medical supply would be a further one month. The number of patients benefited from this supply will be 750 patients (سبعم ئه وخمسون مريضا)

As for Ibn-Baladi Hospital, the load of patient is increasing as the economical , nutritional and sanitary conditions of the population this hospital draines is deteriorating very rapidly and hospital maintenance is reaching a standstill due to shortage in spare parts.

As for Al-Mansour Paediatric Hospital, again the load on outpatient and inpatient are increasing alike and getting increasing the number of chronic cases and childhood malignancy, the availability of anti-cancer drugs and the newer generation of antibiotics making the patient care a very difficult task with increased mortality and morbidity. It is a very frustrating situation for the medical staff. Cooling system are out of oder requiring unavailable spares and with IRAQI Summer setting in; you can imagine the working condition for both patients and staff what they are like.

Drainage of hospital is out of order with many blockages leading to an uncrease in hospital acquired infections.

The Central Paediatric Teaching Hospital also suffer from the same disadvantages but cooling and drainage are in better condition despite the collosal load of work on that hospital.

So in general condition, the all three hospitals now are worse than in 1996. Regarding the information about the following hospitals:—

1. Al-Alwiyah Children Hospital; this is a very important hospitals in Baghdad, it serves a large sector of the population in a lower class area with a capacity of about 150 beds. I feel strongly about including it in your program.

2. Kadisiya General Hospital has a paediatric Section, it is situated near Ibn Baladi Hospital.

3. Kerbala Children Hospital is also a large hospital with 120-150 beds and serves a large population in the area of middle Euphrates.

4. Kut General Hospital has a paediatric section about 40 beds.

5. Samawa Children and Obsteric Hospital has 120 paediatric beds in a very depressed area.

Appendix 10: Letter from Dr Khalid Obaydi, 22 May 1997

140

MINISTRY OF HEALTH
MEDICAL CITY
Baghdad - IRAQ

وزارة الصحــة
مؤسسة مدينة الطب
بغداد ــ العراق

No. :—

Date :—

    Dr. Charmouqli will be very pleased to provide you with the required report and he promised to do so in the near future.

    I will do my best to avoid delay in communication to ensure that you receive my letters promptly.

    The M AIC'S Advisory Committee join me in expressing their appreciation and gratitude to the Board for your generous help.

    Dr. Shatha and the family send their best wishes.

Your sincerely,

Khalid H. OBAYDI, FRCS
Consultant Surgeon

MR. H.B. AL-HADDAD M.D.

Consultant
Orthopaedic and Traumatology Surgeon

All correspondence to:

Cromwell Hospital
Cromwell Road
London SW5 0TU
Telephone: 0171-460 2000
Sec. Ext. 5914, Appt. Ext. 5700
Facsimile: 0171-460 5555

Princess Grace Hospital
42-52 Nottingham Place
London W1M 3FD
Telephone: 0171-486 1234
Facsimile: 0171-935 2198
Mobile: 0836 262608

HBAH/cl

17 June 1997

Dear May

Thank you for sending me the Annual Dinner Card. The cheque has been sent to Mr Sabah Mahmoud. As you know I was recently in Baghdad and had the opportunity to visit several orthopaedic clinics and paediatric hospitals. I also gave lectures for the orthopaedic surgeons at the Medical City of Baghdad. My impression from the hospital visit was as follows:

1. In short supply were antibiotics, drugs for heart problems and diabetes. Diuretics and analgesics were also short. The hospital pharmacies were empty. The only drug found was a mild pain killer.

2. To give the patients a general anaesthetic was difficult and sometimes impossible. I understand from the surgeon that sometimes emergency operations are performed using only local analgesic drugs without a narcotic.

3. There is urgent need for oxygen mask adapter. I found in the paediatric hospital with around 30 children only one oxygen mask adapter which was used for 4 children at the same time (½ minute each in turn).

4. A hospital with Emergency Centre and Orthopaedic Department carrying out about 400-500 operations/month has only 30 units of blood in the bank. Blood transfusion is only given in emergency cases just to keep the patient alive. I understand from the surgeon that they lost a great number of patients because of lack of blood.

5. The surgeons use ordinary household thread which is normally used for dress making to operate and this produces over 70% infection.

6. I myself saw children and elderly patients dying from dehydration because of lack of normal Saline.

7. There are numerous blood donors but there is a lack of blood containers to preserve the blood.

Cont/2...

Appendix 11: Letter from Dr Hassan Haddad, 17 June 1997

Cont/...

8. There is a huge need for mattresses in all hospitals. The patient or patient's companion bring their mattress and blankets with them to the hospital.

9. In most of the hospitals the air conditioning units and elevators do not work and are out of order while the thermometers occasionally record 50°C.

10. There is a huge need for bandages, x-ray films, plates and screws for fractures, hip and knee prostheses, ECG machines, CT scanner, laboratory instruments and machinery, and any simple things is taken for granted in the civilised world.

In my opinion the health system is a disaster and I wonder how on earth they are able to keep the system going until now. I do not believe that European doctors and surgeons are able to work for a short time under such circumstances. The above points are only part of what I have seen. The whole thing is simply unbelievable. I hope you will be able to integrate part of these points in your speech.

With kind regards.

Yours sincerely

Mr H B Al-Haddad MD
Consultant Orthopaedic & Traumatology Surgeon

IRAQ'S HEALTHCARE SYSTEM: HOPE OR DESPAIR?

by Dr. Maya Al-Memar

Iraq's healthcare system, once viewed as one of the best in the Middle East with extensive and well developed primary, secondary and tertiary facilities, has been stretched to its limits. After 10 years of UN sanctions, war and ongoing violence in the current climate of political instability, the healthcare system continues to struggle, which led to Dr. Waleed George, chief surgeon at Al Sadoon Hospital in Baghdad to describe it as "the worst healthcare system Iraq has ever known." (Medact Iraqi Health Update 2006)

Some progress has been described; Immunization campaigns sponsored by the UN and US have resulted in MMR and polio vaccinations for 5 million and 3 million Iraqi children, respectively. Unfortunately, despite these numbers, a UNICEF study published in April 2007 found that immunization rates are declining due to lack of access to primary healthcare facilities. The report states, "About half of Iraq's districts (60 out of 116) are reporting immunization coverage of less then 80 per cent." (Medact Iraqi Health Update 2006)

Iraq is suffering from a humanitarian crisis, with children, as the most vulnerable members of society, continuing to be hit the hardest. A UN-IRIN (UN Office for Coordination of Humanitarian Affairs – Integrated Regional Information Networks) report in May 2007 showed that there has been a 150% increase in mortality rate of Iraqi children since 1990; child mortality in under 5 year olds is currently 125 per 1,000 live births, where in 1990 it was 50 per 1,000. In comparison, the child mortality rate for the Middle East and North Africa region is 53 per 1,000. Other health indicators used to assess the quality of health in countries are equally bleak; maternal mortality ratio is 294 per 100,000 live births while for the Middle East and North Africa region it is 183 per 100,000. It has been shown that 30% of mortality in children under 5 is

due to pneumonia and diarrhoeal disease in Iraq (UN-IRIN May 2007).

Child malnutrition rates have increased from 19% before 2003 to 26% now. Combined with poor sanitation, the fact that 43% of Iraqis live in absolute poverty and that Iraq's exclusive breastfeeding rates are low at 12%, altogether increasing children's susceptibility to disease and illness and further propagating the spread of infectious diseases ('Rising to the humanitarian challenge in Iraq', Oxfam July 2007). Child malnutrition in itself also affects recovery from disease.

A UNICEF report also highlighted how children are not only suffering physically, but also emotionally and mentally from the stress and trauma of growing up in a conflict zone. 70% of Iraqi children have been shown to suffer from post traumatic stress disorder (Report on the Situation of Children in Iraq, April 2007). This has all been recently highlighted in a report, 'Rising to the humanitarian challenge in Iraq', published by Oxfam in July 2007. The report added how 92% of children are also showing learning difficulties.

The report also addressed some of the exacerbating factors that have added to the deterioration in the provision of healthcare services in Iraq. Concerns about security and ongoing violence have had a multifaceted effect, with healthcare professionals unable to attend work or even being forced to flee the country. The exodus of doctors and hospital staff has led to a collapse in basic services. A study of the humanitarian conditions in Iraq by the Red Cross and Red Crescent states that approximately 2000 medical personnel have been killed, 12000 have fled and 250 have been kidnapped since 2003 (ISRCRC: Final report: Emergency Appeal November 2005-January 2007; issued April 2007). The exodus of medical personnel has had a devastating effect on the Iraqi health sector. Hospitals are understaffed and inexperienced medical residents

Appendix 12: 'Iraq's Health Care System: Hope or Despair', by Dr Maya Al-Mamar, MAIC Newsletter, 2007

undertake operations and procedures they are not qualified to perform.

Conflict has also made it difficult for patients to access healthcare. Dr Mazin Al-Jadiry, Consultant Paediatric Oncologist at Children's Welfare Teaching Hospital in Baghdad, who in June 2007 undertook training at the Alder Hey Hospital in Liverpool as part of MAIC's training program, was able to give us an insight into this. He described how families would often abandon further treatment of their children with cancer due to fear of reaching the hospital safely, as well as severe poverty and being unable to afford the treatment.

The issue of security has also made it difficult to provide humanitarian assistance and also affects the distribution of medical supplies.

Dr Al-Jadiry described the difficulties in providing basic healthcare with limited resources and in unsanitary conditions with poor infection control measures. Basic medical supplies are unavailable. Until 2006, invasive painful procedures, such as lumbar punctures, were carried out without anaesthetic. MAIC donated local anaesthetic to the hos-

A 13 year old amputee at the Basrah Prosthetic Centre, August 2007.

pital, which Dr Al-Jadiry reports has made a significant difference. Storage of medical supplies is difficult due to lack of functioning refrigerators and chilling rooms. Lack of basic equipment, such as centrifuges used to process blood test results and reagents needed for this, also affects delivery of healthcare. At the Children's Welfare Teaching Hospital, one x-ray machine, manufactured in 1979 and since repaired, is available. No computed tomography (CT), magnetic resonance imaging (MRI) or other diagnostic imaging is available.

Dr Al-Jadiry also described the very low staff to patient ratio, which ideally should be one doctor for every 30 new patients. Currently only one doctor is available for every 125 new patients. This makes it difficult to deliver good clinical care, and provide the emotional support often needed by children. In the face of these difficulties, recognising the importance of play for children, the hospital team organised a number of social activities for children in the hospital, for example, a drawing competition funded by the KRSF through MAIC.

MAIC continues in its aims to assist in improving the health of children by sending much needed medical supplies and equipment. The exodus of doctors has highlighted the need for further training of health professionals working hard in Iraq. MAIC hopes to continue its training program to update and improve practice whilst also helping to minimise the potential of further intellectual isolation of Iraqi health professionals.

Despite our ongoing struggle in these endeavours, the main obstacle to improving health service in Iraq remains the issue of security. Despite their personal experiences of the current difficulties, Iraqi doctors in Iraq, like Dr Al-Jadiry, remain optimistic and motivated to make change. Through hard work and determination, MAIC will continue to assist these professionals in their noble efforts.

5

145

MAIC held a Forum on the Health of Children in Iraq at the Royal Geographical Society in London on 3rd May 2005. This was an opportunity for doctors working in Iraq to share their experiences and discuss the current health situation and how the war and sanctions have influenced the diseases they encounter. The panel was moderated by Mr Robert Mabro CBE, a MAIC trustee and included four speakers: Dr Hussein Malik and Dr Ali Rasheed, who benefited from our short term training programme, Dr Jawad Khadem Al-Ali, consultant oncologist at Basrah Teaching Hospital, and Ms Lindsay Hillsum Channel 4 News International Editor.

Dr Hussein Malik described how poor nutrition, a decline in educational enrolment and attendance, unhealthy lifestyles, high numbers of deaths from accidents and violence, and deterioration of preventative health programmes have contributed to the decline in the health of the Iraqi children. Poverty, poor sanitation and lack of uncontaminated water supplies have further added to this. Although since 1990 communicable diseases have not reached endemic proportions, infectious diseases remain the main cause of death in children, with acute respiratory tract infections and diarrhoeal diseases accounting for most of these. Dr Malik also noted an increase in typhoid, measles and mumps amongst the cases he sees.

He also reminded us that Iraq used to have one of the best health services in the region, but believes that budget cuts, neglect and poor management over the last fifteen years have taken their toll on health services. This is further compounded by the fact that training of health professionals was neglected and professionals were academically isolated from the outside world and so unable to improve medical practice. Dr Malik also described the need, following the recent war, to renovate and develop damaged and looted medical buildings, rebuild infrastructure, re-organise the pharmaceutical sector and eliminate drugs shortage, training medical staff and tackle the main causes of communicable and other diseases. He concluded by saying that there has been significant progress made recently, with the rehabilitation and reopening of seventy five hospitals and nearly all primary care clinics that were damaged or looted in the war. In addition, public health programs have been re-established and national immunisation programmes organised.

Dr Jawad Khadem Al-Ali talked about the effects of post-war environmental contamination on health in Iraq.

He described how the drying of the marshes in the South and chemical contamination in the form of depleted uranium, used in the recent wars, have affected the environment and changed the spectrum of diseases seen in Basrah, where he works. Dr Al-Ali found increased rates of cancers, particularly leukaemia in children, increased rates of birth defects, changes in the pattern of cancer presentation, and the appearance of uncommon phenomenon, such as familial cancer clustering and double and triple cancers in one patient. Moreover, the shortages in treatment and nursing care have aggravated the problems.

Dr Ali Hameed Rashid spoke about the effects of war on the mental health of Iraqi Children. He described the results of studies he and his colleagues conducted in Iraq, examining the many different ways in which Iraqi children are exposed to traumatic experience. These experiences include the death from armed conflict of one or both parents, siblings, other relatives, and friends, especially where death was witnessed by the child. Direct and indirect exposure to traumatic events, such as car bombs, forced evacuations from family homes and cities, abductions and other violent experiences lead to severe and disabling psychological damage. The continuous exposure to trauma, along with other factors such as, the absence of qualified mental health aid, escalation of the violence, the poor understanding and handling of their psychological problems at home and school and the absence of psychosocial support has made traumatic disorders in children not only more widespread but also more severe.

Ms Lindsay Hillsum, Channel 4 news International Editor, also spoke of her experiences in Iraq at the event. She described numerous moving stories of people she had encountered during her visits in Iraq; stories of heroism and tragedy.

MAIC would like to take this opportunity to thank all those who spoke at the Forum and who came to support the event in particular our experts on the panel: Professor William Yule, Director of the Child Traumatic Stress Clinic, Maudsley Hospital, London as well as Dr Penelope Brock, Consultant Paediatric Oncologist at Great Ormond Street Hospital, London.

MAIC would also like to thank the International Arab Council Charities Fund (IAC) for generously sponsoring the event and all our kind donors who made this event possible.

5

Appendix 13: MAIC's Forum on the Health of Children in Iraq, MAIC Newsletter, 2005

30th October 1996

Mrs. May Al-Daftari
M.A.I.C.

Dear May Al-Daftari,

I am pleased to inform you that we have received your medical supplies which all the paediatric hospitals in Iraq were in great demands for them.
I started with my colleagues to distribute the consignment to the paediatric hospitals as listed in your letter of June 19th 1996.

We send samples for the Quality Control Centre as you know the regulations here, after that I took permission for the use, then I informed all the hospitals for starting using the drugs. Meanwhile all the hospitals have received their medical supplies, except there was a slight delay in Basrah delivery, but today they have sent people to receive it.

Everybody was happy for your and M.A.I.C. help as there were shortage of most of the items.

As your request, the following information you would like to know:

- I enclose the acknowledgement of the receipt.

- The date of actual use of medicines by the hospitals was 23.10.1996.

- An estimate duration of the medical supplies at current usage rate is one month.

- An estimate of patient's number that will benefit from the use of medicines are roughly 15.000 pt.

- We enclose the list of medicine as requested by the paediatric hospitals for the future shipments.

On behalf of the Iraqi Children, we would like to thank you and M.A.I.C. Members and Prof. S. AL-TABAQCHALI for your kind help and efforts.

Dr. Shatha and the family send you special regards.

Your sincerely,

KHALID H. OBAYDI, F.R.C.S.
CONSULTANT SURGEON
BAGHDAD – IRAQ

Appendix 14: Letter from Dr Khalid Obaydi, 30 October, 1996

**MINISTRY OF HEALTH
MEDICAL CITY**
Baghdad - IRAQ

بسم الله الرحمن الرحيم

وزارة الصحـة
مؤسسة مدينة الطب
بغداد ــ العراق

No. :—

Date :— July 5th 1998

Mrs. May Al-Daftari
Chairman
Medical Aid for IRAQI Children
11 Berkeley St., Mayfair, London W1X 6DU.

Dear Mrs. May Al-Daftari,

Thank you very much for your letter of June 1st'98. I would like to inform you that the medical consignment and the three incubators have been received on the 30th May,98. Since then, many contacts have been made with the hospitals concerned per your letter: I managed to deliver the incubators to the following hospitals:-

1. Al-Tifil Al-Markazi Paediatric Hospital.
2. Al-Mansour Paediatric Teaching Hospital.
3. Al-Kadhmiah Hospital.
4. Al-Samava Paed. Hosp.
5. Dar Al-Tamrith Newmate Hosp.
6. Al-Anbar Paed. Hosp.
7. Al-Mousil Paed. Hosp.
8. Baghdad Teaching Hospital (Newmate Unit).
9. Al-Habibia Paed. Hosp.
10. Al-Hidia Paed. Hosp.

The following hospitals promised me to come and collect their incubators:-

1. Kurkuk Paed. Hosp.
2. Basrah Paed. Hosp.
3. Al-Forat Al-Awsat Najaf Hosp.
4. Nasria Paed. Hospt.
5. Amara Paed. Hosp.

Regarding the Medical Consignment, I have managed to deliver them to the following hospitals:-

1. Al-Mansour Teaching Paed. Hospt. (12 big Carton + 3 small Carton).
2. Al-Tifil Al-Markazi Paed. Hospt. (10 big Carton + 2 small Carton).
(The hospitals will inform me about the number of the items in each Carton).

3. Al-Kadhmia Paed. Hosp.   (11 big Carton + 2 small Carton).
4. Al-Samava Paed. Hosp.   (11 big Carton + 2 small Carton).
5. Al-Nasria Paed. Hosp.   (11 big Carton + 1 small Carton).

The total number of the Cartons was 64. In my next letter, I will send you the details of the items of each hospital.

So many thanks for you and for m a i c Board Members and on behalf of the Children of IRAQ, I wish to express their sincerest thanks for your help.

Shatha and the family send you their best wishes.

Yours Sincerely,

KHALID H. AL-OBAYDI, F.R.C.S.
CONSULTANT SURGEON
D.G. SADDAM Medical City.

Appendix 15: Letter from Dr Khalid Obaydi, 5 July 1998

Balmore Park
Upham
Hampshire
SO32 1HQ
tel: 01489 897890
fax: 01489 896215

29th April 2003

May Al-Daftari
Medical Aid for Iraqi Children (MAIC)
26 Old Brompton Road
London
SW7 3DL

Dear May

MEDICAL AID FOR IRAQI CHILDREN

You have asked me to write to you to confirm that the pharmaceuticals and medical equipment that you have provided will form part of the relief shipment that we are sending to Iraq tomorrow night. Please accept this letter as confirmation that this is so and, in this respect, you will note that I have copied you on the delivery instructions showing where your consignment should be delivered to Heathrow Airport. You have also asked me to confirm that your consignments will be delivered to the hospitals nominated. I would like to tell you that we have been assured, by the Coalition Forces that this will be the case, and I have asked Lillan at Durbin plc to make sure that the goods are marked accordingly.

Best wishes

Yours sincerely

JOHN CAULCUTT

Registered Office:- Balmore Park, Upham, Hampshire, SO32 1HQ
Registered in England:- No 1479936 VAT No:- 411 7168 70
A Watermark Group Company

Appendix 16: Letter (fax) from John Caulcutt, Watermark, 29 April 2003

MEDICAL BRANCH
1 (UK) ARMD DIVISION
OP TELIC
BFPO 645
IRAQ

Mrs M Al-Daftari
Medical Aid for Iraqi Children
26 Old Brompton Road
London
SW7 3DL
United Kingdom

2nd May 2003

MEDICAL AID DELIVERY 2nd MAY 2003

I would like to take this opportunity to thank you very much for your generous donation of Medical Aid which we received this morning at Basrah International Airport from the Virgin Airlines flight.

You will pleased to hear that we were able to arrange immediate safe storage of the medicines and equipment and they will be moved very shortly to the intended recipients.

I know from my conversations with local doctors and specialists that the drugs and equipment are vitally needed and will be very much appreciated.

Many thanks

pp

COLONEL J T GRAHAM
COMMANDER MEDICAL
MIDDLE EAST

Appendix 17: Letter (fax) from Colonel John Graham, 2 May 2003

MINISTRY OF DEFENCE
OLD WAR OFFICE BUILDING WHITEHALL LONDON SW1A 2EU

Telephone   020 7218 6966   (Direct Dialling)
                    020 7218 9000 (Switchboard)

MINISTER OF STATE FOR
THE ARMED FORCES

D/Min(AF)/AI/4/34/1   1) December 2003

Dear Ms Al-Daftari

I am writing in response to your 5 November letter to Hilary Benn about medical supplies
to be distributed to hospitals in Iraq. My officials have looked into the situation surrounding
the distribution of the supplies you mentioned and it has taken some time to verify the facts
of the matter.

As Colonel Graham said in his letter to you, the UK Divisional HQ received the medicines
and equipment on 2 May, stored them safely and undertook to arrange for their passage to
the intended recipients. However we have no record of any undertaking to deliver
equipment or medicines to hospitals across Iraq or obtain receipts for their delivery.
Indeed had we been asked to do so we could not have given such an undertaking since
there would have been no real way for us to deliver supplies to Baghdad at that time. The
fact that you believe you had such an undertaking from Watermark is something you would
need to take up with them.

Nor are we able to verify the exact amounts received or delivered. Whilst I appreciate that
your contribution was obviously made in good faith, our usual experience is that charities
would normally have representatives on the ground to oversee the safe delivery of their
donation. In this case the supplies arrived with British Forces in Basra unsolicited. Rather
than have them returned to the UK, Colonel Graham made his best endeavours in the
difficult circumstances pertaining at the time to have them delivered to the intended
recipients in good faith. He went to great lengths to make this happen at a time when he
and his staff were heavily engaged in their military duties.

Where the hospitals were located in other parts of the country Korean Food for the Hungry
took possession of the supplies for onward despatch. Where they were in south-eastern
Iraq we made other ad hoc arrangements to get the supplies there. I should caution that is
unrealistic to expect that the MAIC supplies could be tracked in the same way they are in
the UK, particularly in an environment where looting was a regular occurrence and there
was an ever-present danger to military personnel. Colonel Graham's letter was sent the
day after the end of major combat operations. That is partly why we would not have
undertaken to ensure their safe delivery. As there is no way of knowing what was received
by individual hospitals we clearly cannot verify their claims that some has gone missing. I
note your comment that earlier shipments encountered no problem, but I suggest that
circumstances were rather different.

Mrs M Al-Daftari   Private Office
MAIC
26 Old Brompton Road
London SW7 3DL   INVESTOR IN PEOPLE

Appendix 18: Letter from The Rt Hon. Adam Ingram MP, 15
December 2003

I am sorry not to able to offer more assistance but it appears that your enquiries may be more fruitful if they were directed at the charity involved in distributing your supplies as well as the hospitals which received them.

Yours sincerely

Adam Ingram

The Rt Hon Adam Ingram MP

Mrs M Al-Daftari
MAIC
26 Old Brompton Road
London SW7 3DL

Recycled Paper

m a i c
MEDICAL AID FOR IRAQI CHILDREN

The Rt Hon Adam Ingram MP
Ministry of Defence
Old War Office Building
Whitehall
London
SW1A 2EU

22 December 2003

Dear Mr. Ingram,

Thank you for your letter of 15 December 2003 in response to my letter to Hilary Benn of 5 November 2003 regarding MAIC's missing medical supplies. I very much appreciated the time you spent in verifying the facts of the matter. I would also be grateful if you could kindly shed light on the delivery of our medical supplies to the Basra hospital as the area is under British authority.

Colonel John Graham the British medical officer in Basra at the time informed us that MAIC's medical supplies were moved to the Basra hospital on 10 May 2003 as mentioned in his communication of 19 May 2003 (copy enclosed). After the delivery of the supplies, MAIC re-established contact with its team of doctors in Iraq and was informed that a significant amount of the supplies assigned to hospitals were missing. Moreover, on 18 July 2003 Peter Troy (DFID) wrote to MAIC and sent paperwork from the Basra hospital listing the supplies received from MAIC. The list MAIC received totalled in value £29,367.50 accounting for only 44% of the total supplies value £65,496.99 sent to the Basra hospital (see copy of invoice from Durbin Plc enclosed). To facilitate Colonel Graham's communications with the hospitals, I repeatedly stated in my letters the name of MAIC's contact at each hospital. In the case of the Basra hospital the contact was Dr. Jawad Khadem Al-Ali. As Basra has been under British control, I did not think it was unreasonable to expect Colonel Graham to arrange safe delivery of our supplies to the Basra hospital and to acquire a delivery receipt.

I would further wish to comment on the following points raised in your letter;
Regarding the delivery instructions and request for receipts, I included delivery instructions with the medical supplies which were assigned to five paediatric hospitals. I also wrote several times to Colonel Graham on 19 May 2003, 28 May 2003, 23 June 2003 and 10 July 2003 kindly asking him for hospital receipts and repeating the delivery instructions.

You have kindly stated that usually charities have representatives on the ground and that MAIC's supplies arrived in Basra unsolicited. MAIC was approached by Virgin Atlantic to send medical supplies on Virgin's humanitarian flight to Iraq. We hesitated before agreeing as at the time there were no lines of communication with our doctors in Iraq and we were waiting to re-establish contact. We were told at the time that the coalition forces had asked Virgin to put together a humanitarian aid flight to Basra and hand over the supplies to the coalition forces for distribution to hospitals. In order to accept Virgin's offer to send MAIC's supplies on that flight, I asked Watermark, the company representing Virgin

26 Old Brompton Road • London SW7 3DL • Tel: 020 7581 2727 • Fax: 020 7581 2767 • E-mail: info@maic.org.uk • Website: www.maic.org.uk
Registered Charity No. 1044222

Appendix 19: Letter from May Al Daftari to Adam Ingram, 22 December 2003

Atlantic, to confirm that the coalition forces would be responsible for the safe distribution of MAIC's medical supplies. I received confirmation on 29 April 2003. (copy of Watermark letter enclosed). MAIC's supplies were sent on the flight with complete paperwork which included the UN/DTI Export Licence, Durbin's packing lists and distribution instructions.

Regarding Korean Food for the Hungry, the agency used by the coalition to distribute our supplies, I wrote to Colonel Graham asking him for the agency's address and contact details. Unfortunately he did not respond. Colonel Carmichael who took over the post from Colonel Graham sent us their address and email in Korea. I emailed them on 30 July 2003 but got no response.

As for your advice to contact the assigned hospitals, I did so at the time and received the lists of missing supplies from another two hospitals apart from Basra.

The total value of the missing items is £98,784.49 divided as follows;
Basra Paediatric Teaching Hospital. Total amount of supplies missing is £36,129.49
Al-Mansour Paediatric Teaching Hospital. Total amount of supplies missing is £28,680.95
Central Paediatric Teaching Hospital. Total amount of supplies missing is £33,974.05
I have prepared a complete file with all the relevant documents and communications should you wish to review it. MAIC is seeking compensation from the British Government for the amount of £98,784.49 in order that the charity can replace the missing supplies.

As a Trustee and Board Member of MAIC, I am saddened that so much effort was put into this humanitarian aid consignment to help sick and injured children. So many fundraisers nationwide have helped us during this past year by raising funds towards this large consignment which totalled in value £201,410.98. (Copy of the total invoice from Durbin plc enclsosed).

I hope you give this grave matter further consideration as delays are causing more hardship and suffering to sick children.

Yours sincerely,

May Al-Daftari

Request to Donate Medical Assistance

Medical donations must be reviewed and approved by the International Aid Committee before being brought into Iraq. The preferred form of donation is financial. Other donations must meet a recognized need and should improve the capacity of the Iraqi health system to provide for its people. Donations must follow accepted international standards.

Date of application: _____

Organization / Country: _____

Name and contact information of your representative:

Name _____

Phone _____ Fax _____

Email _____

Type of donation (select all that apply):
☐ Financial
☐ Medical supplies
☐ Medical equipment
☐ Vehicles
☐ Communications and information technology
☐ Infrastructure rehabilitation
☐ Pharmaceuticals
☐ Other (specify) _____

Please attach a detailed list and description of the proposed donation to include the following as applicable: Activities and experience in Iraq, proposed future activities, list of donated items, date of availability, mode and route of transportation, storage needs, security requirements, and all coordination that has been completed to date.

Aid Committee Determination:
☐ **Approve**   ☐ **Decline**   ☐ **Approve with modifications**
Official / Date _____

Ministry of Health   **WHO**   **UNICEF**   **ORHA**

Appendix 20: New Regulation Form by Iraq International Aid Committee (IMAC), to Donate Humanitarian Aid in Iraq

MAIC

From:	"Sawsan Sayyab" <sawsan_sayyab@yahoo.co.uk>
To:	"MAIC" <info@maic.org.uk>
Cc:	"David Tarantino" <tarantinod@orha.centcom.mil>
Sent:	09 June 2004 07:28
Subject:	Re:

Dear Dr. May

Greetings , I have recieved your mentioned email , but since The IMAC have already handed all its files & responsibilities to the ministry of Health / The International affaires department since the mid of March 2004 , so I forwareded it to them .
Please kindly contact them for any further information , or contact Dr. David Tarntino who is cc on this reply ,
My regards
Sawsan Al- Sayyab

M 'C <info@maic.org.uk> wrote:

> Dear Mrs Sayyab,
> Kindly confirm receipt of the email I sent to you on 28 May 2004.
> Kind regards - May Al-Daftari

MAIC

From:	"The Iraqi Ministry of Healthy" <iraqimoh@yahoo.com>
To:	<info@maic.org.uk>
Cc:	<tarantinod@orha.centcom.mil>
Sent:	07 July 2004 07:56
Subject:	Application to IMAC for approval

Dear all

Referring to your proposal regarding medical supplies and pharmaceuticals.kindly notethat your proposal has been approved by MOH with some modification includes: the pharmaceutical should accompanied by certification with full qualification and should be from a dependable origin. This should be done with cooperation with storage and distribution office/custom department of our ministry.
We seize this opportunity to express our gratitude to your organization showing attitude to contribute for assistance of Iraqi children.
Dr. Ramzi R. Mansour
Director of Int. health depart./MOH

MAIC

From:	"Tarantino, David (O-5)" <tarantinod@orha.centcom.mil>
To:	"MAIC" <info@maic.org.uk>
Sent:	09 June 2004 15:19
Subject:	RE: From MAIC

Basically submit your proposal to the MOH as you have done and Dr. Sawsan described; they will review for approval (as they are doing now for your current proposal)

For now, you should keep me in the loop N as I can monitor, forward, facilitate .

Dave Tarantino

> From: MAIC [mailto:info@maic.org.uk]
> Sent: Wednesday, June 09, 2004 5:31 PM
> To: Tarantino, David (O-5)
> Subject: From MAIC
>
> Dear Mr. Tarantino,
> Ms Sawsan Al-Sayyab kindly informed me that IMAC has already handed in the files to the Iraqi Ministry of Health. She also confirmed that she forwarded my email of 28 May 2004 regarding MAIC's next medical shipment to you.
> Could you please advise what the new regulations are concerning receiving aid from British NGO's.
> Best wishes - May Al-Daftari

Appendix 21: IMAC Emails Advising MAIC That It Had Handed Over Its Files to Iraq's MOH after March 2004

WITH GOD AT WYDALE HALL (North Yorkshire)

The sheep in white coats stand silent on the hill,
There is no breeze, the leaves on the trees are still,
Amongst the flowers the butterflies flutter their wings,
The land is warmed by the sun which summer brings.

A bird, white-winged, soars high above the trees,
The rain-refreshed flowers invite the buzzing bees,
Upon the green lawn a blackbird comes to rest,
Then up and away to the safety of its nest.

Surrounded by stillness and silence God is revealed,
This beauty is given by God, our souls are healed,
But Man has made of this Earth a field of blood,
Where Iraq's dead children lie in a sea of mud.

Man's cancer-carrying bombs have brought disease,
There are no scenes of peace, no flowers, no trees,
Here grieving mothers stand in the noon-day sun,
In rubble where once their children played for fun.

God, when will the men of power give up this game
Played out with bombs and bullets in Christ's name?
When will they take the blindfold from their eyes?
When will they heed the Iraqi mothers' cries?

John Stephenson

Appendix 22: Samples of Poems from Booklets by Reverend John Stephenson in Aid of MAIC

WAR BE DAMNED

One day this planet Earth will be no more,
Now there is no peace, no end to war,
The Iraqi people have seen their children killed,
Many tears have been shed where the innocent blood was spilled.

When will there be an end to the killing game?
When will the men of power show some sign of their shame?
When will they repent and admit that their wars are unjust?
When will their deadly weapons of war be turned into dust?

Your rule is at an end, you men of power,
The world awaits the rule of peace to flower,
Where the human rights of people have first place,
Where mercy, pity and love have a human face.

(Rev) John Stephenson

 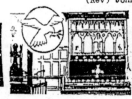

HEAVEN AND HELL

The sky is blue, my garden is lit by the sun,
The harsh fierce winter has gone, now spring has begun,
The starlings and blackbirds are pecking away at the bread,
Soon summer will come, the proof that cold winter is dead.

Meanwhile inside my house on the T.V. screen
There are faces of starving children, a terrible scene,
These are the poor, denied their daily bread,
Unwanted, unseen where the rich man's friends are fed.

This is a world where war and greed co-exist,
A world which is ruled by fear and the iron fist,
Where the poor of the Earth are trampled underfoot,
Where mercy and peace cannot thrive, nor justice take root.

(Rev) John Stephenson

158

Biochemist on mission to get vital drugs to Iraq

Penicillin pioneer, 91, is still fighting to save lives

By Alison Bartlett

NEARLY 60 years after an Oxford biochemist played an instrumental role in discovering penicillin, he and his wife are sending a donation of the antibiotic to Iraq.

Dr Norman Heatley, 91, of Oxford Road, Old Marston, Oxford, is the last surviving member of the Oxford research team that discovered penicillin could be used to fight infection during the Second World War.

Most people credit Sir Alexander Fleming with discovering it but, although he observed its power to kill bacteria, he never discovered its life-saving potential.

It was Oxford scientists, working under Prof Howard Florey, who first trialled penicillin on patients at the Radcliffe Infirmary in 1941.

Despite Dr Heatley's ingenious efforts at cultivating it during the war, using hospital bed pans, baths and milk

MERCY MISSION: Dr Norman Heatley talking to May Al-Daftari

churns, production could not keep pace with demand and US drug firms had to be persuaded to develop a means of mass manufacture.

In 1990, Dr Heatley finally received recognition when Oxford University awarded

him an honorary doctorate in medicine. Now he and his wife, Dr Mercy Heatley, are working with the charity Medical Aid for Children in Iraq to donate penicillin to the country's hospitals.

On Tuesday they met

chairman May Al-Daftari, who explained how to complete the complicated paperwork required.

Medical drugs are free from sanctions but, before they can be sent, supplies are scrutinised by Government

and United Nations committees to ensure they cannot be used to develop weapons of mass destruction.

Dr Mercy Heatley has been writing to the Foreign Office for six years highlighting the plight of Iraqi doctors forced to work with inadequate drug supplies. The psychologist is within dying seven per cent of her income tax on a private income, which she claims goes to military defence, to draw attention to her campaign.

Dr Mercy Heatley said: "There are four times as many cases of cancer in children in Iraq as there were before the Gulf War.

"The drawn-out procedure of scrutinising drugs often means doctors do not have the right combinations of drugs available, so children in Iraq are dying."

She said many children also died from drinking contaminated water. The penicillin would cure them of life threatening infections.

alison.bartlett@nqo.com

Appendix 23: Article on the Heatleys: 'Penicillin Pioneer 91, is Still Fighting to Save Lives', Oxford Mail, 21 February 2002

You are warmly invited to the
Wedding Ceremony of

Nicola Lynne Kainey Greenwood
and **Martin George Wyatt**

at Princes Street United Reformed Church, Norwich
on Sunday September 18th 2005 at 10.30 a.m.
Church open: 9.45 a.m., Orchestral prelude: 10 a.m.

Light refreshments available afterwards at the Church

Informal attire

No presents - just your presence.
Donations to Medical Aid for Iraqi Children:
"We have everything, they have nothing"

R.S.V.P.:
"Martin and Nicola's
Wedding Celebration",
c/o Head In The Clouds,
13 Pottergate,
Norwich,
Norfolk,
NR2 1DS

Appendix 24: Wedding Invitation for Nicola Green and Martin
Wyatt, Benefitting MAIC, 18 September 2005